Filmag 20 14

INDIGO & OPIUM

This book is dedicated to the memory of my parents,
Ian and Ruth Macnair, whose marriage in 1918 forged the link
that connected these two remarkable families together.

INDIGO
& OPIUM

Miles Macnair

BREWIN BOOKS

BREWIN BOOKS
56 Alcester Road,
Studley,
Warwickshire,
B80 7LG
www.brewinbooks.com

Published by Brewin Books 2013

A CIP catalogue record for this book is available
from the British Library.

ISBN: 978-1-85858-517-8

Printed in Great Britain
by Gomer Press Limited.

Acknowledgements and Sources

Several members of the Hills/Evans families and their descendants wrote memoirs that were never published and I am deeply grateful to those of the present generation who have kindly let me have access to them. Some have also done their own research into their ancestors and have generously allowed me to quote from their efforts. The same applies to many family portraits and photograph albums. I wish to record my sincere thanks to the following; Christopher Evans, Phylidda Mould, Joy Neal, Genia Conroy, Archibald Chalmers-Hill and Marie-Louise Luxemburg (Savi family).

There are fewer and less widely dispersed primary sources for the Dent family and so I am particularly grateful to my cousin Nicholas Dent who has devoted so much time to his family researches. The story of the Dents in India and China would have been impossible without his generous help. Philip Law who contributed the Dent Family entry into the 2004 version of the Oxford Dictionary of National Biography has kindly shared some of his researches into the archives of the former Barings Bank. My thanks also go to Gerard Dent for allowing me to reproduce the portrait of John Dent MP in his possession and for access to various Dent letters.

The Dent saga is intricately involved with that of Jardine, Matheson and Co. whose vast archives are now in Cambridge University, thanks to a chance discovery in China by a roving scholar in the 1930s, Gerald Yorke. He himself wrote the draft of a book based on this material, combined with his own erudite commentary. This was never published, due to an embargo by the Keswick family, but Gerald's son, John Yorke, has very kindly allowed me to quote from one of the rare manuscript copies still in existence.

My final thanks go to my beloved wife, Juliette, for travelling round the world with me in my quest for ancestral roots, for deciphering my family's handwriting and for wise revisions to early drafts.

Preface Notes

Values and currencies

The Indian currency was then, as now, denominated in Rupees, **Rs**. The nominal value of the Rupee in the mid 19th century was about two shillings (10 pence sterling).

Trade with China was conducted in silver. The Chinese demanded payment in Spanish (Mexican) Dollars, represented by the **$** symbol in this book. The value of this coin fluctuated according to supply and demand as well as its intrinsic, bullion worth but at the period of this book it was approximately five shillings – or 25 pence sterling.

In return, the Chinese paid for imported goods with silver *taels*, small bars of silver minted into a variety of shapes of which dished 'boats' or 'shoes' were the most common. The weight of silver in each *tael* also varied from region to region but averaged between 33 and 38 grams, or about 1¼ ounces. *Taels* were supposed to be made from 99.9% silver, but coastal traders in particular had to be careful about debased metal and counterfeit *taels,* an important role for the *shroff* on each ship.

Weights of both indigo and opium were most commonly denominated in *chests*, tea in avoirdupois *pounds* and heavier commodities in *piculs*, about 133 lbs and based on the maximum load that two men could carry on a shoulder pole.

To convert £ sterling values to those of the early 21st century involves a multiplier of about 70 times.

Place names

Names of places in India and China are written in the form used at the time. Where these have changed, the modern name is recorded in brackets against the first mention only.

The English spelling of Chinese names varies from one source to another which may account for any inconsistencies.

Maps and Plates

Pictorial Credits

1 Phylidda Mould. 2, 24, 25 Genia Conroy. 3, 4 Joy Neal. 5*, 13, 14*, 18, 20-23, 28-36, 38-39, 44-48, 63-64*, 69-72, 74-81 Author. 6 Le Fevre Gallery. 9 Deutsches Textil Museum, Krefeld 16044. 10, 11, 12, 15, 16, 17, 26, 27, 40-43 Christopher Evans. 37 London Films. Front Cover, 50, 61 © National Maritime Museum, Greenwich, London. 49 Gerard Dent. 53-56, 59-60, Nicholas Dent. 57 Macau Museum; photo by Martyn Gregory Gallery, London. 58, HSBC Archives Hong Kong. 65 Hong Kong Museum of Art. 68 © Durham University Museums.

* These paintings were commissioned by the author from James Williams, Robin Barnes and David Wilson respectively.

Introduction

In the middle of the 19th century, two commodities dominated the mercantile economy of British India. One was indigo and the other, more contentiously, was opium. Exports of these two plant extracts accounted for more than half the value of all exports from Calcutta and the money raised from the profits made, and the duties and sales taxes levied on them, fuelled the growth of the British Empire. Equally important to the British economy, opium sales to China were vital to balance a massive negative trade imbalance with that mysterious country. The growing addiction of the English for tea, then only produced in China, was putting serious strain on the finances of the Treasury. To satisfy one addiction it was politically necessary to encourage another.

Indigo, the rich blue dye, was a boon to the fabric industries of the world, praised for the depth and lustre of its colour and applauded for its resistance to fading and the fact that it held fast to every type of fibre treated with it. In its heyday it was more valuable, ounce for ounce, than gold. Everything about it seemed to be a positive blessing, though in the years of the industry's decline around 1860 it would lead to a 'peasant's revolt' in Bengal that had long-lasting political implications – the foundation of the Indian Congress Party.

Controversy, however, always surrounded opium. For some people, both doctors and patients, it was a uniquely powerful medicine that cured diseases resistant to all other treatment, while its ability to suppress pain had no parallel. But to other people it was an addictive drug that could ruin men's lives. Its history is clouded by violence, conflict and even international wars.

Two families were dominant players in the dramas surrounding each commodity. Both made huge fortunes, fortunes that would then be lost through a shipwreck in one case and a financial crash in the other. James Hills and his relations became the kings of the Indian indigo industry and the Dent family were one of three that dominated the opium trade into China. All previous books about this trade and the 'Opium Wars' have been based very largely on the extensive Jardine, Matheson archives; this is the first that concentrates on the drama from the Dent perspective.

These two families, the Hills and the Dents, linked by a marriage in 1918, are my ancestors and this book is their story.

Book One

THE HILLS SAGA

Chapter 1

Beginnings in the Borders and a shipwreck

Soon after midnight on Thursday August 9, 1821, Captain Alexander Scott collapsed onto the bunk in his cabin utterly exhausted. **[Plate 1]** He had been on deck for nearly 36 hours, battling his ship against a tropical storm in the Bay of Bengal. Now he handed over command to his first mate and went below to snatch a few hours sleep. The *Lady Lushington* was a three-masted barque of 634 tons, a typical square-rigged East-Indiaman and this was her fourth trip to India. With a high poop, upright prow and a broad beam, she was not built for speed but seaworthiness combined with a capacious cargo-space.

On this occasion she was carrying a draft of soldiers heading for Calcutta (Kolkata), a total of 65 passengers and crew, and had stopped to re-provision and take on fresh water at Madras (Chennai) on August 5. Among the passengers, and entrusted to his special care, was Captain Scott's nephew and my great-great-grandfather, James Hills, who had recently celebrated his 20th birthday. James Hills was the second of nine children and the eldest son, born to a family of respected tenant farmers on the Cheviot Hills in the Border Country around Jedburgh.

This was the homeland of the reiver families, the no-man's-land between England and Scotland that had been disputed for centuries. Powerful local warlords had built up their fiefdoms here, families like the Scotts, the Montagus and the Douglases. To the confusion of historians, there were also two particular families with very similar names, the Kers of Cessford and the Kerrs of Ferniehurst. They could trace their ancestry to a pair of brothers in the 14th century who had fallen out and subsequently 'the two houses maintained a jealous rivalry'. [1] All these families were perpetually raiding each other's land and castles, rustling cattle and disputing the entitlements to rival Earldoms such as Buccleuch, Lothian, Ancram and Roxburghe. Blood-feuds rankled from one generation to another; scores once thought settled would re-emerge in bloody vendettas. [2] Occasionally families would intermarry for dynastic reasons and once in a while members of the younger generation would fall in love and make illicit liaisons, like Shakespeare's Montague family and their rivals the Capulets. And it seems that just such a youthful infatuation lurked in the ancestral background of young James Hills.

James Hills' grandmother was Margaret Ker who had been baptised in the parish of Wilton, near Hawick, on March 3, 1749, [3] and there is a web of mystery over how she came to marry James Hills' grandfather, also called James Hills (Snr.). Margaret Ker was the daughter of General Walter Ker and his wife Bessie Scott, and it was he who would later in 1807 start a ruinously expensive, and ultimately fruitless, court case against Sir James Innes over the entitlement to the Dukedom of Roxburghe. [4] Family legend has it that Margaret had eloped with a younger scion of a branch of the Buccleugh Scotts, maybe called Archibald, by whom she became pregnant. They may even have undergone some form of 'Gretna Green' type marriage service, though if they did the 'marriage lines' were destroyed by his family. [5] He had then gone off to war and been killed. Margaret Ker's pregnancy became an embarrassment that might open old wounds and it is believed that it was through the intervention of the dowager Duchess of Buccleugh that one of their tenant farmers, namely James Hills Snr., was persuaded to marry her in the late autumn of 1770. On the 28th of April, 1771, she gave birth to Archibald Hills, young James Hills' father. It was widely known that *a curious difference in features and build and in temperament and tastes distinguished this son from the later born children.* [6] Of these there would be five who survived infancy. [See Appendix B]

When his father died in 1795, Archibald Hills took over the tenancies at the age of 25 and four years later he married a Miss Elizabeth Scott, whose father Adam Scott of Nisbett was described as 'a country gentleman of the family of the Duke of Buccleugh'.[7] This would have been seen as a rather good marriage and probably came with a handsome dowry, and during the years between 1801 and 1814 he and his wife had nine children. One of their descendants owns a charming, rather naive, portrait-group of the seven young girls and their two brothers painted by a local artist. **[Plate 2]** But as time went by it seems that Archibald Hills became less conscientious towards his farming and estate management duties as he enjoyed his enhanced social status and 'took to the bottle'. The tenancies of the two farms at Harestanes and Copland cost him £1,800 per annum to the Marquis of Lothian, from whom his brother, John Hills, rented Morebattle Farm for a similar amount. But there had been an economic slump following the end of the Napoleonic Wars in 1815 and the price for farm products had plummeted once imports from the continent were resumed.

Another reason why Archibald Hills lost his money was because he had been generous in his support of his grandfather's great court case, perhaps understandably so because he would benefit considerably if General Walter Ker had succeeded in his claim to the Dukedom of Roxburghe. The court case dragged on over seven years, made a fortune for the lawyers and was a scandalous sensation in its time. One of the reasons it became so drawn out was the immense complexity of the family relationships involved over centuries, combined with the legal interpretation of various wills and deeds. Once it failed, however, and General Ker's relations had been impoverished, it becomes irrelevant to the ongoing story of the Hills family. But it makes a gripping tale in its own right, one with a very contentious conclusion, so it is included as Appendix D later in this book.

After the failure of the Roxburghe claim, Archibald Hills was facing financial ruin. He was forced to give up his tenancies at Harestanes and Copland and move to a much humbler role at Halterburn farm in the Cheviots, near the 'gypsy' town of Yetholm, where his two boys are recorded in the school register. In 1821 it was decided that the eldest son, young James Hills, should leave to seek his fortune in India, prompted no doubt by stories his uncle Captain Alexander Scott told about this golden land of wealth and opportunity. There were no other family connections to draw on as far as I can gather, so it would be a bold and risky step into the unknown.

As his parents bade their sad farewells, Archibald Hills promised his wife that he would abstain from alcohol until their beloved son returned – a vow that he kept until his death in 1836, even though he would never see his eldest son again.[8] At least they would have been comforted to learn, at least six months after the event, that young James Hills had eventually reached India and survived the storm of August 9, 1821. But only just.

At 4 am that morning, Captain Alexander Scott was awoken by a dreadful crash of splitting timber as the *Lady Lushington* was driven onto a reef. The ship had been holed below the waterline and very quickly started flooding. Captain Scott's first concern was for the safety of his young nephew, who couldn't swim, and so he lashed him to a hen-coop and threw him over the side with the parting words *'take your chance with God, me lad'*.[9] The reef was about half a mile off shore and somehow or other James did manage to survive being tossed around in the breakers until he was washed up on the shore of Orissa. [Plate 5] He would in fact be one of 43 survivors including Captain Scott himself, who filed a report to Messrs. Curling & Dummet about the shipwreck four days later at Pentacottah. Attached to this report was a letter signed by four army officers commending Capt. Scott for 'the excellent conduct he displayed during that melancholy and trying event', while stating that he should not be blamed for the loss of his ship, which was entirely due to his orders not being obeyed.

Now the family myth, on which I was brought up, went on to say that young James Hills, near the point of death and with no possessions apart from his waterlogged clothes, was rescued from the surf by an Italian doctor named John Angelo Savi. He was then nursed back to health by Dr Savi's wife and three young daughters, and when he recovered, he made his way to Calcutta, got a job in a firm of indigo brokers and made a quick fortune. A few years later, he returned to the Savi family and wooed and wed the youngest and most beautiful of the Savi daughters, the 17 year old Charlotte Marie Savi.

The earlier part of the legend is, I am sorry to say, a complete fantasy but the last sentence is absolutely true – James Hills and the ravishing Charlotte Savi were indeed married in Calcutta on the 6th of June, 1831. But the reality of what had actually happened to James Hills in the ten years between his very wet and traumatic arrival in India and his wedding is itself a story of considerable enterprise and romance. Escorted by his uncle on the final leg of their journey to Calcutta, he had been taken on as a writer by the firm of Alexander & Co., *but he was indiscreet enough to fall in love with the daughter of the head of the firm and was promptly banished, whereupon he went to Murshidabad (the site of one of the businesses owned by the Savi family) – where he made a rapid fortune in indigo.*

Chapter 2

The Savi Dynasty

So who were the Savis and how could one make a fortune from a textile dye that was a natural plant extract? The answer to the second lies in some rather unusual botany, massively labour-intensive agriculture and processing, and a world-wide demand for an intense blue dye that had mystical and practical properties like no other. And this will occupy the next chapter.

But to answer the first question we must delve back into a little more genealogy and tales from a turbulent period in the history of India, when England and France were trying to establish trading posts and often coming to blows over territory.

The Savis originated from the island of Elba, with one branch of the family migrating to Florence where they seem to have prospered. There was once a Palazzo Savi in that city and several monuments to members of the family still exist. [10] Marco Savi (1695-1765) came from the Mugello valley to the north-east of Florence and one of his sons, Antonio Savi (1720-1806), joined the navy of Tuscany, which also owned Elba, and rose to the rank of Admiral. On his retirement to Elba he married and fathered a large family including a son christened John Angelo Savi in 1765. **[Plate 3]** This young man trained as a doctor and seems to have worked his passage out to India in 1784 as a ship's doctor/surgeon.

The ship's destination was the port of Pondicherry, which had been under French rule since 1673. It had been a centre of conflict between British and French interests, represented by their respective East Indian Companies, for decades. During the series of Carnatic Wars which began as an off-shoot of the War of the Austrian Succession (1740-48) the French besieged and captured the British trading port of Madras (Chennai), which had been originally founded by the British in 1644 as Fort St George. This was restored to British administration at the Treaty of Aix-la-Chapelle in 1748, in exchange for the town of Louisberg in Canada. Fighting flared up again in the Seven-Years War (1756-63). General Robert Clive led the army of the East India Company to victory at the Battle of Plassey in 1757, which established British rule over the province of Bengal in the north-east of India, and enabled him to turn his attention to unresolved issues in the south-east, the Carnatic region behind the Coromandel Coast. This included the princely states of Hyderabad and Mysore and the less well defined regions of the unruly Marata tribes.

In 1761, in revenge for the earlier humiliation at Madras, Clive captured and sacked Pondicherry. Clive's success in these campaigns was largely due to the fact that he was actively supported by units of the British army and navy sent out from England by the then Minister for War, William Pitt (the elder), unlike his French opposite number, even though the French East India Company was notionally under the direct control of the French Government in Paris.

By 1763 the young King George III was three years into his reign and beginning to assert his own authority. He saw himself as a peacemaker, loathed his prime-minister the Duke of Newcastle, whom he sacked along with the belligerent William Pitt, and appointed his tutor and mentor the Earl of Bute in his place. The Seven-Years War was concluded that year by the Treaty of Paris, and one of the clauses, seen by many in England as too conciliatory, restored Pondicherry to the French. One particular French officer who saw considerable active service on the sub-continent against the British was Andre Francois Corderan. Born in Paris in 1742 although of Breton stock, he had enrolled when a young man as a cadet in the 'Artillerie des Indes', and his subsequent service record mentions '4 combats, 2 battles, 5 sieges and 2 sea-fights'. He had been captured by the English in 1761 during the siege of Pondicherry, taken to England and then repatriated as part of a prisoner exchange. He was back in India shortly afterwards. In 1778 the French were on the attack again, believing that British colonial influence had been dealt a fatal blow by the American War of Independence and the surrender of General Burgoyne's army at Saratoga. But they underestimated the determination of the Governor General of the East India Company, Warren Hastings, and when Pondicherry fell once more to British arms in 1778, Captain Corderan again found himself a prisoner.

After some dithering, the Madras government chartered a ship, the *Sartine*, to convey the Governor of Pondicherry, M. Bellecombe and his wife, plus the French garrison officers, to Marseilles under a flag of safe-conduct – 'cartel'. Ten months into the voyage and rounding Cape St Vincent in early 1780, the *Sartine* was challenged by a British man-o'war, HMS *Romney*, whose Captain was more concerned at seeing a mass of French officers on the deck than the validity of the 'cartel' flag. This, he suspected, was a ruse and opened fire, killing his opposite number on the *Sartine*. After she surrendered, a boarding party established the facts of the case and she was allowed to proceed, somewhat battered, to Marseilles. The French immediately filed a protest with the British Admiralty demanding a court-martial and this document bears the signature of Corderan among those of the other officers. [11]

The American War of Independence had turned into a global conflict, with France recruiting the active support of Spain and the Dutch Republic. Sea battles were fought in the West Indies, Spain annexed Florida, Gibraltar was besieged and the harbour of Trincomalee on Ceylon (Sri Lanka) was lost to the French. By 1783 the main protagonists were militarily exhausted and economically ruined, so diplomatic feelers for peace resulted in the Second Treaty of Paris being signed the following year. A few islands were swapped, new understandings on spheres of influence were reached and trading ports returned to their previous occupants – including Pondicherry. And to command the garrison there, Andre Corderan, now Colonel, set sail from France with his wife and nine year old daughter Elizabeth. (He was later promoted to be a Marechal by Napoleon Bonaparte and a gold pencil presented to him by the Emperor was at one time in the possession of Thomas Savi's family.) This happened to be the boat on which Dr. Angelo Savi was the ship's doctor/surgeon and during the long voyage he entertained and was in turn entranced by the pretty, flaxen haired Elizabeth Corderan. **[Plate 4]** On arrival at Pondicherry, they promised to keep in touch and there were fond farewells as the young Doctor headed north to start a completely new career.

It seems that he may have had some private means because the next thing that is known about him is that he had started an indigo plantation and set up a processing plant in Bengal at a place called Oolooberiah in the district of Nuddea (Nadia). This was close to the French trading post of Chandernagore (Chandannagar), about 20 miles north of Calcutta on the River Hooghly, which had originally been granted to the French by the local Mughal ruler in 1673. [12]

Apart from his indigo interests, Dr Angelo Savi was still practicing as a doctor for local rajahs and his knowledge of European medicine may well have been a highly prized asset. By 1789 he had chartered a ship called *La Maria* which he loaded with Indian goods, including chests of his indigo, for export to Rangoon in the neighbouring country of Burma across the Bay of Bengal. His first port of call was Pondicherry where he spent four weeks taking on more cargo and almost certainly renewing his friendship with the Corderan family. He also spent time administering to the health of a shadowy character, an Englishman called William Caldwell who was, according to a file discovered much later in the Government records at Calcutta, acting as an undercover agent for the EIC. [13] And just to add to the mystery, Dr Savi himself was travelling under the 'nom-de-guerre' of Sage – the literal French translation of Savi. [14] *La Maria* set sail from Pondicherry in May with Dr 'Sage' and his patient William Caldwell, who was hoping to achieve a cure for his liver complaint by taking the waters at the mineral springs of Pegu outside Rangoon. [15] Having delivered his human cargo into the hands of the local EIC agent, a Mr Busby, and traded his merchandise with local merchants, Dr 'Sage' set out to return to India.

How he achieved this and precisely when is unknown, because *La Maria* had been wrecked in Rangoon harbour when a typhoon had blown in.

But return to Pondicherry he certainly did, to ask for the hand of the girl he had fallen in love with seven years earlier. On October 2, 1790, Dr John Angelo Savi married the sixteen year old Elizabeth Corderan and together they returned to his Indigo factory in Bengal to set up home and start a large family. Emelia Savi was born in October 1792, and over the next 24 years they would have eight sons – two of whom died as infants – and another four daughters, the youngest, and reportedly the prettiest of the 'Savi beauties' being christened Charlotte Marie Antoinette Savi in December 1813.

Over the years, the extent of Dr Angelo Savi's indigo operations had expanded considerably, the acreage under cultivation in the Nuddea district had increased enormously and the number of processing factories had grown to seven. These all needed management and supervision and it seems very probable that he recruited the ambitious and enterprising young James Hills as an assistant and junior partner around 1824. James Hills had already absorbed the techniques at the trading end of the indigo business, even if his apprenticeship with Alexander & Co. had ended somewhat abruptly. Like modern day dealers on the currency and commodity exchanges, he had learnt about arbitraging and margins and the factors that affected prices. And how to recognise the difference in quality of indigo grown in distinct regions and on different soils. Now he would have to master the complexities of organising many thousands of local peasants – *ryots* – to grow the crop and process it to meet the rapidly expanding demand from buyers around the world. Exports of Bengal indigo to London in 1782 amounted to 25,000 lbs, a figure that had increased to 4,400,000 lbs by 1795 and 7,650,000 lbs (estimated to be worth £2.5 million) twenty years later. Fortunes could be made by men of enterprise though the risks were daunting. [See Appendix A]

Chapter 3

The Mystic Indigo

Of blues, there is only one real dye, indigo.
William Morris.

Indigo, with its rich, intense blue colour, is unique among natural dyes for being totally 'fast', clinging tenaciously to any fibre soaked into it. It is impossible to wash out, and it works equally well on all types of fabric; wool, silk, flax or cotton. Unlike other natural dyes, it is resistant to fading and if one looks at old tapestries, it is very noticeable that it is the blue that has survived much better than any other colour. To the dyer, indigo was the equivalent of lapis lazuli to the artist. **[Plate 9]**

Various species of the indigo plant are found across the world. The northern European version, *Isatis Tintoria*, is commonly known as woad, and it was the extract from this plant that ancient tribes used to paint on their skin to frighten their enemies. It is, however, a poor, pale thing compared to the version that grows in warmer climates, *Indigofera Tintoria*, which was first discovered growing wild in India. Early traders took it to North Africa and the West Indies, while the Dutch took it to South-East Asia. But it was in the alluvial plains of East Bengal that it really thrived. The plant is a perennial shrub, related to the mustard plant and lucerne, and in the wild can reach a height of over six feet, but the best quality dye comes from second year growth. For peasant farmers it offered, potentially, a far more profitable return than any other crop, though there were hazards. First of all the seeds had to be purchased from the planter and this usually involved borrowing money from local money-lenders who were notoriously unscrupulous over the interest they charged. Preparation of the soil started immediately after the autumn harvest and demanded months of breaking up the baked surface, hoeing and weeding to ensure that a fine tilth was ready for the first sowing in March once the soil had started to warm up again. Autumn sowing was risky but if successful produced the best yields of all. Germination took only a few days but the seedlings were very delicate and a cold snap could prove fatal.

The correct, slightly alkaline, moisture level at this stage was also crucial but after that the plants grew rapidly during the lengthening days of scorching sunlight until the arrival of the summer rains. If the monsoons failed, which occurred about once every twenty years, the crop would be ruined. The final imponderable for the farmer was that the price paid by the planter for the harvested crop was not guaranteed in advance and fluctuated with the market price offered by the Calcutta merchants. But in the years between 1820 and the 1850s there was prosperity to be shared at all levels as world demand exceeded supply and prices for high-quality indigo escalated in a virtuous spiral.

Growing indigo was one thing; extracting the dye was quite another, and a weird, complicated process it was, combining delicate technical skills with great manual effort.

The harvested leaves were taken by the farmer to the planter's 'factory' where they were weighed, assessed for quality and paid for. **[Plate 7]** Then the leaves were bruised in a mill and loaded into tanks of water where they were allowed to ferment until greenish foam was produced. The timing of the next stage, transferring the liquor into the oxidising vats was critical. Here the surface had to be 'thrashed' for hours with wooden poles by men standing waist deep in the vats, a process that aerated the liquid and caused sediment to precipitate to the bottom. **[Plate 8]** Finally the waste liquid was run off into the nearby river and the sediment was extracted and filtered through presses before being cut into cakes and laid out on matting to dry. [16] But not too much. This was another stage that needed close supervision to ensure that the cakes ended up with the consistency of bars of soap rather than little bricks.

One of the most important outlets for indigo in Britain was cloth for the uniforms of officers and other ranks in the Royal Navy [See cover illustration.] [17] In France the same applied to military uniforms. Visibility and the ability to distinguish friend from foe was of prime importance on the battlefield in the days of black powder for muskets and artillery, which is one of the reasons the British Army chose the prominent red. It is perhaps of interest that the dye used for the 'redcoats' was derived from the roots of the madder plant, also extracted by a fermentation process. Unlike indigo, it quickly faded in sunlight to a pinkish-brown, but it was much cheaper than the red dye used for army officers' uniforms, the very expensive product from crushed beetles of the cochineal species.

Chapter 4

Neechindepur and Children

The Savi family were the kings of the indigo industry in Bengal. Their eldest daughter Emilia (1792-1858) was unlucky in her first two husbands who both died young, but in 1820 she married George Barton who was the senior partner in the Calcutta trading agency of Gisborne & Co., a firm that James Hills would later use as his main selling agents. (Barton also had his own plantation operation in the state of Bihar.) Five of the Savi sons became planters; John Henry (1797-1852), Thomas (1801-1880), Joseph Alexander (b1805), Julien Robert (b1806) and James (1816-1867). The second daughter Cecelia married Charles John DeVerrine who was another planter with his operations in the administrative region of Jessore, (Thomas Savi would marry Charles's sister as his second wife.) The third of the 'Savi beauties' Elizabeth Teresa (1810-1897) married yet another planter called Francis Loweth in 1826 when she was just 16, gave him five children and then did a bolt with an official in the Civil Service of East India Company. This caused a considerable scandal, though she did eventually marry him when she learnt that her first husband had died in London in 1869.

> *My mother was one of a large family of brothers and sisters, one of whom she was not allowed to have any intercourse with, as she had run away from her husband with a young civilian.*

James Hills **[Plate 10]** proved to be an excellent manager for his new employer while charming his way into the heart of the Savi's youngest daughter. She was sent to be educated for three years in England and, on her return, James Hills and Charlotte Savi became engaged. She was seventeen and the portrait painted for her engagement confirms that she was stunningly beautiful, with large eyes, a mass of dark hair and a long, graceful neck. **[Plate 11]** Elsewhere she was described as 'having both grace and beauty ... and the impersonal loveliness of some Madonna.' [18] They were married on June 6, 1831, and exactly nine months later she gave birth to their first child who was christened Archibald in honour of James's own father. The following year, with his father-in-law's blessing, James Hills took his wife and baby son off to start his own indigo operations some distance away from the district of Nuddea, in the Kishnaghur (Krishnagar) region of East Bengal, most of which is now in Bangladesh.

East Bengal is one vast delta for the mighty River Ganges. Nowadays the main flow exits into the Bay of Bengal at Dacca but this was not always so. Up until the 16th century the primary channel was what is now called the River Bhagirath which in turn became the River Hooghly that passes through Calcutta. But the banks of the rivers were ill defined and the Ganges spread its fingers over the entire flood plain as the slow moving waters meandered their way towards the sea. Silt piled up in some areas while seasonal floods would force new channels, like the Jalani and the Marthabhanga. Once the 'big shift' eastwards took place, defining the present route of the Ganges past the town of Kustia, the geography of the delta settled down, leaving a large number of low-lying islands of fertile soil surrounded by shallow, virtually currentless waterways and isolated ox-bow lakes. The early inhabitants were seasonal, nomadic squatters but after the risk of annual inundation had diminished, villages grew up on the banks of the islands.

After the collapse of the Mughal empire in 1764, the land in East Bengal was initially taken over, and exploited for their own short term enrichment, by the *zamindars* who had been the local administrators and tax collectors for the Mughal emperor. The system was formalised by the EIC, following a series of devastating famines, by the introduction of a series of Permanent Settlement Acts at the end of the 18th century that gave landlord rights to the *zamindars* in exchange for a fixed annual payment. Although these amounts were initially calculated on a reasonable percentage (11%) of the rental income expected to be gathered from local farmers in a normal year, they lacked any flexibility to allow for periods of flood or drought. These Acts were designed to give incentives for investment in infra-structure projects like roads and bridges, though another consequence was that farmers were encouraged to grow profitable cash crops, like indigo, rather than food crops for local consumption. The Acts also imposed strict penalties on any *zamindar* who failed to fulfil his annual quota of dues to the EIC. Default led to an immediate auction of the land involved to the highest bidder, and in many cases, particularly following the decline of the indigo industry after 1857, this would turn out to be a banker or merchant or indeed a British Civil Servant, resulting in a large number of absentee landlords.

One of the Savi sons, Thomas, had already opened the first indigo factory in the Kishnaghur region at Moisgunge and it was on another nearby island, close to the village of Kapashdanga, that James Hills decided to build his house and set up the

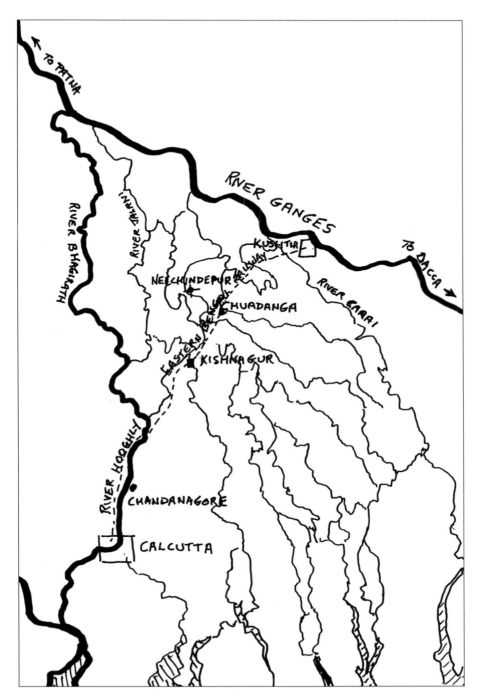

Map 1. Sketch map of the Ganges Delta, showing the principal waterways and the location of Neechindepur in relation to Calcutta and Kishnagur. Also the route of the Eastern Bengal Railway and the station at Chuadanga.

first of his own operations. Over the next 20 years, he would build up ten concerns with over 32 separate factories, concerns that would involve well over 60,000 *ryots* cultivating, harvesting and processing indigo on his behalf. There is no doubt that he was a caring employer, always referring to the *ryots* as 'his children' and they in turn held him in high regard. All this made him an immensely wealthy man.

The house he arranged to have built was an extremely imposing mansion in the classical neo-Palladian style; he called it Neechindepur, which meant 'the house without anxiety' in the local dialect, though in family records it was always referred to by the less attractive abbreviation of 'Neech'. **[Plate 12]** The total estate amounted to 22,000 acres, of which 17,000 were leased and 6,000 owned freehold. [19] Although it relates to a slightly earlier period and a completely different property, the painting in **Plate 6** is interesting for a number of reasons. [20] It combines, in retrospect, two events relating to the purchase of land in Bengal by William Dent and his brother Capt. John Dent; first the handing over by a *zamindar* of the original purchase documents and then the grand house that was later constructed on the site. Another interesting, and coincidental, feature about this painting is that this Dent family were also ancestors of mine – see Book 2, 'The Dent Saga'.

The building materials for Neechindepur would have been brought up north on river-craft from Calcutta, a journey that took at least three days by boat even though the direct distance on a map was only about 60 miles. Set back one hundred yards from the river bank, Neechindepur had a long verandah running along the front of the upper storey that housed the bedrooms, each with a fine view over the surrounding countryside. The flat roof above was supported on a line of eight stone columns while there was a bow-fronted colonnade around the main entrance. On one end of the mansion was a large block of servants' quarters and there were spacious stables for horses at the rear, enough for 70 according to Sir Henry Cotton. And an elephant.

The years between 1830 and 1857 were the 'golden years' for indigo, particularly after the East India Company's longstanding trading monopoly was rescinded by the British Parliament in 1833. The planter families in this early era lived on site and generally took a personal, paternal interest in their *ryots* while also acting as the local magistrates. The vast scale of the industry can be judged by the fact that in the 1840s there were between 330 and 400 indigo factories in Bengal, Bihar and Jessore, while approximately 3½ million people were engaged in production over an area of 1.3 million acres. [21] Output from Bengal alone amounted to around 9 million pounds per annum, or 35,000 chests each weighing an average of 280 pounds.[22] Ounce for ounce, it was more valuable than gold. Indigo was of huge significance to the economy of British India and, in value terms, represented nearly half of all exports from Calcutta. [23]

Charlotte Hills bore her husband eleven children and it is somewhat of a miracle, given the generally unhealthy climate of East Bengal, that ten of them survived infancy and lived to see old age. [See Appendix A] They were as follows; Archibald (1832-1896), 'Jimmy' (1833-1919), John 'Jack' (1834-1902), George (1835-1895), Robert 'Bobbie' (1837-1909), 'Lizzie' (1838-1897), Charlotte 'Totty' (1840-1916), Veronica Harriet (1844-1931)*, 'Charlie' (1847-1935) and 'Emmy' (1848-1938). The only fatality was a little boy born in 1842 who only survived for six months. He had been christened Elliott Macnaughton Hills after one of James Hills' best friends, a *nabob* who had made a fortune as a director of the East India Company. As we will see later, the child's death was perhaps an omen of misfortune ahead when James Hills had to mortgage his property to Macnaughton.

The five elder boys were all packed off at a young age to be educated back in the UK, firstly in Edinburgh and then at the military cadet school of the EIC at Addiscombe in Croydon. Three of them did take up careers in the Indian Army, with great distinction as we shall see, though Archibald, the first-born, returned to India to become an indigo planter in his own right, at Patkabaree in the Murshidabad region of Nuddea. He made so much money in his first season that he returned to England and blew the whole lot on renting a grouse-moor in Scotland and partridge shooting in Norfolk. Things were not so good in subsequent years and his plantation was in debt for the rest of his life. Sir Henry Cotton described him as 'the best of good fellows, but his lot fell, unfortunately, on the decaying days of the industry.' [24] Archibald was a renowned hunter of wild boar, 'pig-sticking', contributing to a text-book on the techniques of this dangerous sport that became the standard work on the subject. [25] He is credited with being the first man to have 'stuck' a leopard from horseback. His younger brother 'Bobbie' became an indigo broker with Thomas & Co. in Calcutta, to be joined later by the youngest brother of them all, the debonair 'Charlie' Hills who, as we will see later, may go on to father a film-star.

Soon after 'Totty' was born in 1840, James Hills took his wife back to Scotland on a visit to Edinburgh. There they stayed with his widowed mother (his father had died four years earlier) and spent the holidays with their sons who were then at the Edinburgh Academy under the care of his sister Jackina and her husband, Robert Barton. (This couple are referred to by VHP in her memoirs as 'Uncle & Aunt Barton'.) They also visited another of his sisters, Elizabeth, who had married William Ingram, the then owner of the 200 acre Copland farm, next door to Harestanes, the two farms once tenanted by her father.

---

* *Author's note.* She was always known in the family as 'VHP' or 'Granny Pugh' and from now on the abbreviation will be used to differentiate her from her own daughter Veronica.

In the Scottish connections, there had been rather a prejudice against 'James's foreign wife', being a Roman Catholic, but all vanished before her and she was acknowledged by one and all to be the most adorable creature in mind and body that they had ever known.[26]

On their return to India they were accompanied by James's other sister 'Tomima' who was aged 36, rather deaf and had never married. Neechindepur was a happy home for the Hills daughters and their young brother Charlie. By 1850, the elder daughters would have had their own ponies and the two younger children would have their play-time on the edge of the river supervised by their ever attentive ayahs while they romped around 'Emmy', the baby of the family who was now a toddler.

A great joy was our evening ride on the elephant – always before we mounted the howdah, two brown cottage loaves were brought which my mother gave the elephant, while I gave it two sponge cakes. Then she used to tell me bible stories, and it grieved me that the goats were the bad people and the sheep the good, as I much preferred the dear goats when they were brought in to be milked.

I remember the occasional treat of being allowed down to dinner in the long room and having a sip of champagne from my father's glass. He sat at the top of the table with my mother on his left. After the dinner downstairs, it was an awesome flight through the big empty rooms and stairs, with visions of cats' eyes at every corner, until I reached my ayah who was waiting to put me to bed. And then the cries of the jackals to lull me to sleep.

VHP also recalled the occasional trip to Calcutta to visit her French grandmother, Elizabeth Savi,

My mother and I used to go in the budgerow and it took about a week there and back. [27] *She gave me sweets and toys and lived at the south end of Chowringee Road, and she used to smoke a jewelled hookah.*

James Hills was often away, overseeing the work of his widely spread factories and plantations, but his return would always be an occasion for rapturous joy as he was greeted home by his beautiful young wife and the younger children. But then, in the month of April 1850, a dreadful tragedy struck 'the house without anxiety'.

Chapter 5

A Tragedy and Another Shipwreck

When troubles come, they come not single spies, but in battalions.
Macbeth

VHP was now aged 5, the naughty one of the family and her mother's pet. When she was 70, she started writing her memoirs for the benefit of her numerous grandchildren and recalled with anguish what happened next.

My mother's illness was very short – rheumatic fever. Aunt and Uncle Hills had come over from Katcheekatta, their factory, and to make them more comfortable, my mother had turned out of her room and given it to them. My father had gone to Kishnagur on business. He dreamt he sat on the veranda at home with my mother when a big black bird came between them and hid her from him. He got up and called for his palkee.

Nearing Neechindepur, he met his assistant, Mr Sibbald, and asked "All well at home?" "All well" he replied "but Mrs Hills was not down yesterday." So he arrived to find her on her deathbed. Doctor Archer was sent for from Kishnagur and I remember leeches were applied; also the smell of laudanum that I recognised years later. I was of course banished from her room most of the time, but I used to hang around watching for a chance to steal in and kiss her.

Then on the last day I was made to go down all by myself to that long room and I was given my favourite dish – minced scallops and rice. Then all at once there was a cry throughout the house and I heard my mother was dead! Oh I fancy I was dazed and stupefied, but when I knelt at my aunt's knee to say my evening prayers and it came to 'God bless Mamma', the floods came and my Aunt, who loved my mother as everyone did, soothed me and put me to bed. But not to sleep; I knew too well what those hammering strokes meant and in the morning they took her away.

Charlotte Hills was buried in the graveyard of the little mission church up the river. James Hills withdrew into a state of overwhelming, solitary grief over the loss of the beautiful young wife he had adored since she had been a child, and for quite a long time he could not bear the sight of her children that reminded him all too poignantly of the void she had left behind. So VHP and Charlie were taken away to Katcheekatta, the indigo estate owned their father's brother-in-law, James Hills Jnr, while Emmy was taken care of by Aunt Eliza Savi of Moisegunge. The three children and their aunt Tomima sailed back to the UK in 1851, calling in at St Helena where they *bought quantities of grapes which we festooned around the ceiling of the cabins.* Their father took the shorter route which involved an overland stage across Egypt before sailing up through the Mediterranean from Alexandria. [28] Now the whole family was reunited in Edinburgh and VHP expressed her *great trepidation at meeting my big brothers and sister.* It was here in Edinburgh that James Hills commissioned the composite portrait shown in **Plate 13** which shows all ten children as if they were back at Neechindepur in mourning for their mother – though mischievous VHP, her pet, is trying to lighten the otherwise sombre atmosphere.

Before leaving India, James Hills must have left instructions with his agents, Messrs Thomas and Co., concerning the price he expected for that year's indigo crop on the Calcutta markets. The electric telegraph had not yet reached India so last minute decisions had to be made by those on the ground and it seems that the agents, failing to achieve the target price, decided on the alternative option of sending the entire crop back to England on a single ship that they chartered – without taking out insurance. Somewhere on the journey the ship foundered and was never heard of again. This was an absolute disaster and forced James Hills to return to India as quickly as possible.

> *I do not think that my father's affairs ever quite recovered from this – he got into the hands of Elliott Macnaughton, and had to return to India, though by the time he was home again in 1854/5 he was a rich man once more.*

In just two years he had partially restored his fortune, though at the same time taking on a large debt, and he had appointed a new and very efficient manager, James Forlong. Kling describes him in his book 'The Blue Mutiny' as 'a white sheep in a black flock – a man of liberal views, who knew the value of compromise', contrasting him to other managers who 'unbendingly opposed any concessions to the peasants'. On James Hills' instructions he built the only hospital between Calcutta and Kishnagur and supported two schools, one for lower caste children and one for higher caste students. [29] However, as VHP recalls, his private life was less satisfactory.

> *Mr Forlong was a very lordly and handsome person. Mr and Mrs Forlong were married at Neechindepur though it was not a very happy union. Her temper, I*

hear, was vile and I believe there was just a trace of 'the tar'. I don't know if she died or if they separated by mutual consent.

The indigo industry was still booming and James Hills was outwardly prosperous once more, though if he had been able to read about the work of the British scientist William Perkin and some of the chemical experiments taking place in Germany into synthetic dye production, he might have realised that dark clouds were gathering on the horizon. [See Bibliography, Garfield, S]

Chapter 6

Romantic Interludes and the family goes to war

The years 1854 to 1857 were happy ones for the family back in Scotland. The summer holidays of 1854 were spent in the Highlands, renting a house from Lord Lovat which they shared the first year with the ambitious young James Mackenzie, who James Hills had recruited as one of his managers. (He will recur later in a nemesis role.) When their father returned from India, he took them all to Boulogne in the summer of 1855.

The 'Great Review' took place while we were there, with Queen Victoria, Prince Albert, the Emperor Napoleon and Princess Eugenie. She was such a lovely woman and so perfectly dressed. The camp was miles and miles of tents it seemed to me, and all the officers in uniform and medals in front of the hotel were a great excitement for us.

In the summer of 1856 the whole family, plus James Hills' assistant Mr Sibbald, went to Dieppe where the first fluttering of teenage love began to stir in the girls' hearts.

It was at Dieppe that Mr Sibbald had the indiscretion to fall in love with Totty, who, though only 16 had a wonderful fascination. My father was very indignant at his presumption and he left in disgrace. Totty of course looked upon him as an old man! I suppose he was about 35. I pined in secret, for he was my first love – Totty had quite cut me out and I was nowhere in his attentions.

Dear Totty had no suspicion of the feelings she had aroused, for already she considered herself devoted to young Macadam, son of the Macadam who made the roads and was later knighted. He got a commission in the cavalry and went out to India when he was 17 I think. They were engaged to be married when he

20

came of age. Soon after he went to India, the Scottish business crashed and he lost nearly all his fortune (which was large) and so he wrote to our father to say he was no longer in a position to marry and proposed to break off the engagement. My father accepted this statement but learnt afterwards that Macadam had not meant it to be taken so, though he felt honour bound to allow Totty to give him up. He was a good fellow – handsome, strong and dark, but with an ugly mouth and prominent lips. I used to think that I would not like to be kissed by him!

The following year there was an even greater romance when a friend of 'Aunt Barton', a naval widow called Mrs Jones, had her son Jenkin to stay during his leave.

He was an Engineer officer and met and immediately fell in love with my beautiful sister Lizzie [Plate 20] and proposed to her. Our father was furious – no one in heaven or earth could assume to be good enough for her. However, he went off and exploded to his old friend Elliott Macnaughton, who soothed him down and said that a Captain in the Engineers was good enough for anyone.

So my father gave his consent and Jenkin Jones was asked to dinner, where the poor fellow's confusion was very apparent. He was very shy, and to be suddenly ushered into our large family circle as a marked guest was an ordeal.

The wedding was to take place in due course but then the thunderbolt fell – the terrible news of the Indian Mutiny. Jenkin's leave was of course stopped and he was under orders to leave at once. He pleaded hard to be married before he left and said that if he went he might be given an appointment that could not be left, and then Lizzie might have to go out to India on her own to marry him. So he prevailed and a week's preparation sufficed and they were married at All Saints, Finchley Road. Old Mrs Jones said it was a dismal affair, more like a funeral. Lizzie and Jenkin went to Matlock for their brief honeymoon and in a week he was off.

James Hills now had two sons and a son-in-law involved in what the British call the Indian Mutiny and Indians refer to as the 'First War of Indian Independence'. George, now aged 22, was a Lieutenant in the Engineers and 'Jimmy', two years older, held a similar rank in the Bengal Horse Artillery. **[Plate 15]** His unit was encamped on some high ground, the Ridge, to the west of Delhi, which had been captured by the mutineers, and he was in charge of a troop of guns under the overall command of Major Henry Tombs. On July 9, 1857, the position was guarded by a picquet from the 9th Irregular Cavalry, and the guns themselves were supposedly protected by a troop of about 32 cavalry from the Carabiniers. The action is best described by 'Jimmy' Hills himself, in a letter to his father. **[Plate 17]** This is a rare document since it was written by the participant immediately after the event and not exaggerated or modified in the light of mature reflection.

"The alarm went and off I started with my two guns to a position laid down for them, when, to my astonishment, through an opening on my right, only fifty yards off, dashed a body of cavalry. Now I tried to get my guns into action, but only got one unlimbered when they were upon me. I thought that by charging them I might make a commotion, and give the guns time to load: so I went at the front rank, cut down the first fellow, slashed the next across the face as hard as I could, when two *sowars* charged me. Both their horses crashed into mine at the same moment, and of course both horse and myself were sent flying. We went down at such a pace that I escaped the cuts made at me, one of them giving my jacket an awful slice just below the left arm – it only, however, cut the jacket. Well, I lay quite snug until all had passed over me, and then got up and looked about for my sword. I found it a full ten yards off. I had hardly got hold of it when three fellows returned – two on horseback. The first I wounded, and dropped him from his horse; the second charged me with his lance – I put it aside, and caught him an awful gash on the head and face. I thought I had killed him, but apparently he must have clung to his horse for he disappeared. The wounded man then came up, but got his skull split.

Then came on the third man, a young active fellow. I found myself getting very weak from want of breath, the fall from my horse having pumped me considerably, and my cloak had somehow or other got tightly fixed round my throat, and was kindly choking me! I went, however, at the fellow and cut him on the shoulder; but some cloth on it apparently turned the blow. He managed to seize the hilt of my sword and twisted it out of my hand. Then we had a hand-to-hand fight, I punching his head with my fists and he trying to cut me, but I was too close to him. Somehow or other I fell, and then was the time, fortunately for me, that Tombs came up and shot the fellow. I was so choked by my cloak that I could not move until I had loosened it. (By the by, I forgot to mention that I fired at this chap twice, but my pistol snapped, and I was so enraged that I threw it at the fellow's head, but missed him.)

When I got up, Tombs was so eager to get up onto a mound near us that I only picked up my sword and followed him. After being there some time, we came down to look after the unlimbered gun which was left behind. When we got down, I saw the very man that Tombs had saved me from going off with my pistol. (He had only been wounded and shammed dead.) I told

Tombs, and we went at him. After a little slashing and guarding at both sides, I rushed at him and thrust; he cleverly jumped aside and cut me on the head, knocking me down – not, however, stunning me, for I warded his next cut when down. Tombs, following him up, made him a pass, and up I jumped and had a slash at him, cutting him on the left wrist and nearly severing it. This made him turn round, and Tombs ran him through. He very nearly knocked Tombs over, for he cut through his cap and pagrie, but, fortunately, did not even cut the skin.

I fancy I am indebted to Tombs for saving my life, for although I might have got up and fought, I was bleeding like a pig and, of course, would have had a bad chance. One thing, however, if Tombs had not been there the second time, I should have fought more carefully. It was my wish to polish off the fellow before Tombs could get up to him, that made me rush at him the way I did.

If those horrid Carabiniers had only charged, the 'sowars' would have caught it in style. Our cavalry, I'm afraid to say, have not distinguished themselves, though they have had some good opportunities, but never like that morning. They would have got these fellows in flank and sent them to awful grief, instead of which they bolted (cowardly hounds) leaving not only me and my guns to look after ourselves, but also their own officers, who shouted to them to charge."

For this heroic action, 'Jimmy' Hills was awarded one of the early Victoria Cross medals, as was his commanding officer, Major Tombs, who had undoubtedly saved his life. [30] VHP recalled how her father *nearly burst with pride when Jimmy won the VC at Delhi*, but also how he then committed the indiscretion of having the letter about the action printed in a newspaper; which caused some offence because of the accusation of cowardice by another regiment.

James Hills' second daughter 'Totty' Hills **[Plate 18]** who had been an invalid as a child, married shortly after the family all returned to India in 1860. Her husband was Lt. William George Cubitt of the 13th Native Bengal Infantry, who brought with him the second VC into the Hills family. The citation for his award ran as follows: 'For having on the retreat from Chinhut, on the 30th of June, 1857, saved the lives of three men of the 32nd Regiment, at the risk of his own.' [31] **[Plate 19]** Remarkably, this would not be the last VC to be won by a member of the family. James Hills' grandson, Col. Lewis Pugh Evans, son of 'Emmy', would be awarded the decoration during the First World War in October, 1917, during the Battle of Paschendale, and the story of his heroic action is told later in Appendix E. **[Plates 42 & 43]**

The pent-up anger and resentment that sparked the Indian Mutiny, and the harsh reprisals that followed in its wake, rang alarm bells in London and convinced the British Government that the administration of the 'Jewel in the Crown' of the British Empire needed to be removed from the EIC and placed under the direct control of a new Department of State. But less than two years later another conflict erupted in India that would have devastating consequences for James Hills and the whole future of the indigo industry.

Chapter 7

The 'Blue Mutiny' and
two more romances

The Bengal Indigo Riots of 1859 were the most serious examples of social unrest in India since the Mutiny. The newly appointed Viceroy, Lord Canning wrote; 'For about a week, it caused me more anxiety than I had had since the days of Delhi ... I felt that a shot fired in anger or fear by one foolish planter might put up every factory in flames.' Resentment against the later generation of 'get rich quick' indigo planters, who were far less benevolent employers than the old established families, boiled over and led to local massacres that had to be vigorously suppressed. The attitudes of conflicting interest groups had been polarised. On the one hand there were the planters and their agents, represented by the Indigo Planters Association and a number of bribable, colluding magistrates, while on the other hand there were the fair-minded British civil servants, under the recently appointed and liberal-minded Lieutenant-Governor Sir John Grant, and the increasingly vociferous class of Indian intelligentsia. The third opposition group were the rapidly expanding number of British missionaries, who believed, somewhat duplicitously, that encouraging withdrawal of labour would help promote their own cause. [32]

James Forlong resigned as James Hills' manager over the Government law appointing some white planters as temporary magistrates; he believed, quite rightly, that these powers should have also been granted to certain local Indian *zamindars* as well. The situation was exacerbated by the Santal rebellion (local tribesmen, very largely Muslims, against Hindu moneylenders), five seasons of bad weather and by a collapse in the value of the indigo harvest as the synthetic aniline dyes invented by the Germans moved into bulk production. Indigo slipped down the rankings of Indian exports to only third place with 11%, behind opium (36%) and raw cotton (24%). James Hills returned to India as quickly as he could but it was too late. He had lost a second fortune. He did however stay on unlike many of the established indigo planters who just gave up, and doubled the price he paid his *ryots* for growing his crops. [33]

Back in England meanwhile, VHP **[Plate 21]** had met and fallen in love with a young Welsh barrister who was just completing his pupilage. Lewis Pugh Evans, born in 1837, was the second son of John Pugh Evans JP and Eliza Pugh, of Llanilar in Cardiganshire, west Wales. **[Plate 22]** In later life VHP left a brief pen-portrait of her future in-laws.

My father-in-law was a tall, fine looking man, intellectual and poetical with a gentle and rather hesitant, dreamy manner. (His son Griffith was like him and I always thought that my Herbert also followed that strain.) He came from Ty Mawr, a farm next to Bodtalog, near Towyn, and was I believe a schoolmaster in Aberystwyth when he met and fell in love with and married Eliza Pugh. I understand the old grandfather settled Lovesgrove on them as the marriage dowry. My mother-in-law was his direct contrast. Short and sturdy with rather a massive head and fine features, very active, very commanding – one might almost say domineering.

Lewis, who had inherited his mother's stocky frame and obstinate streak, had been educated at Winchester and then at Corpus Christi College Cambridge. Theirs was to be a long courtship because VHP, and her Aunt Barton, insisted that they could not become formally engaged until he had written to her father in India and they had received his consent, a round trip of almost nine months. When Lewis could finally tell his good news to his family back in Wales, *his brothers and sisters were quite pleased, but I expect I was 'a daughter of hell' to their mother, for I never saw her till I came home from India after we were married. Then she was always very kind and nice to me but, poor dear, when she was parted from her beloved son, it was too much for her and I believe she had a slight stroke.*

Lewis was the second son of six children, his next brother, two years younger, being called Griffith, while the youngest son was a clergyman by the name of David. *I loved David for his warmth to me – Griffith had been brought to meet me once, but I did not care for him much at the time. As I got to know him though, I loved him in after years.* (This was fortunate, because Griffith would marry VHP's youngest sister, 'Emmy', nine years later.) It was always planned that VHP should go out to India in 1863 so Lewis agreed that he would travel out with her. The night before they sailed from Southampton on November 3, 1863, *the Kingston Rowing Club, of which Lewis was captain for two years, gave him a great farewell dinner and presented him with a silver drinking cup, which I desecrated afterwards by using it as a biscuit tin – much to Lewis's annoyance.* The couple were supposed to be chaperoned on the ship by VHP's Aunt Tomima. *Dear old Aunt Hills I always had affection for, in spite of her morose and dour disposition, and I think she was really fond of me. Lewis and I were hardly allowed to speak to one another on board, but we managed to dodge my aunt after dinner in the dim light of the deck as she liked to go to bed very early.*

James Hills came down to meet them in Calcutta and *gave us both a great welcome and quite accepted and approved of my good choice.* VHP then went back with her father to Neechindepur while Lewis joined chambers in Calcutta and quickly established a most promising career. *His remarkable good looks, his riding – for he had joined the polo club – and his rowing reputation, his knowledge of the law and his general ability all earned him a rapid success.* In spite of having other things on her mind, 19 year old VHP did her best to be a good companion and housekeeper for her father. Every Sunday she accompanied him on the short boat-trip up the river to the mission church where he would kneel by his wife's grave and weep silent tears of abject misery. *I did try and control the bazaar accounts after I found 52 chickens put down for one day's soup! But he only said 'my dear child, it is their custom' and so I gave up.* She paid a short visit to Patkabaree to stay with her Uncle Archibald and his wife Emma, who *tried to be kind and motherly but I thought her horrid then as always.*

Lewis was already earning RS.2,000 [34] a month by the following spring and took the opportunity of a court holiday over the Puja Festival to go up to Neechindepur on the recently opened Eastern Bengal Railway that ran from Calcutta to Kushtia on the Ganges, via Kishnagur. [35] There was an intermediate station at Chuadanga, a relatively short ride in a pony-cart or a *palkee* litter from Neechindepur, so now the total journey only took a few hours instead of three days by boat. *Lewis urged my father to give his consent to our being married at Easter. 'Having come all this way for my wife, is it fair to keep me waiting longer, now that I can show that I can provide for her?'* My father said he was a 'devilish obstinate fellow' but accepted his point.

Lewis and VHP were married at the cathedral in Calcutta on March 28, 1864, by the chaplain, Rev. Cave-Brown. *There is no doubt that we were all hard up and I had the scantiest trousseau and the cheapest wedding gown procurable, all made up by the dirzie. Aunt Hills was, I believe, genuinely fond of me, though her affection was rather quaintly expressed in her parting words to me as I was going away after my marriage; 'God bless you my dear child, I hope you will be happy, but I very much doubt it.'* The couple had a very short honeymoon, only three days, beside the river at Titaghur in a bungalow lent them by a friend of her uncle Dr. James Anderson, who was married to her father's elder sister 'Vaire' Hills. VHP described him as *a dear old man, very ugly, with a brick-red face and upright white hair.* He insisted on providing the newly-weds with a very large Indian cook, who they then took with them when they returned to Calcutta and moved in with the Cave-Brown's at their house at the end of Lower Circular Road.

They were living there during the great cyclone of October 5, 1864, which did enormous damage to property, sank 32 ships in the Hooghly delta and caused the immediate death of nearly 50,000 people. [36]

Totty and George Cubitt, with their little son Willie Martin, had come to stay with us on their way to Neechindepur where we were all going for the Durga Puja holidays. We were to have started by the 7 a.m. train and a great discussion took place the night before as to whether we should take provisions for the journey. Tottie, who always did things very comfortably, said 'certainly', so tiffin baskets were ordered and everything got ready for an early start. The weather was threatening but we thought nothing of it till next morning when any thought of starting was an impossibility and all our energies were required to save our house from being blown away. It was a curious house with 5 rooms all facing south, both upstairs and down. The centre one on the ground floor was the dining-room with the drawing-room above, and two others on each side. Room after room of these we had to relinquish, dragging the beds and furniture into the drawing-room and barricading the windows and doors. About mid-day it was at its worst, but it gradually subsided about 3 o'clock and the servants were able to light fires and get us some food.

I don't remember how we managed to spend the night or how we slept, but we were glad enough next morning to start our journey and get away from our dilapidated house. We were due at Neechindepur at teatime, but alas, the train due to start the day before had been blown right over on its side and it took the best part of the day to clear the line. So it was midnight before we reached the station at Chuadanga. We had demolished the contents of our tiffin baskets early in the day, Willy having given a portion to the poor guard and engine driver who had not had food for thirty hours and who were hugely grateful.

[Plate 14]

At Chuadanga there were no palkees or horses, so Lewis went on ahead to the Glassfords while my brother-in-law was left in charge of us at the station. Mr Glassford had gone to bed, when Lewis walked straight in and woke him up and explained our predicament. He at once got up and got hold of coolies etc. and had us conveyed to his house, where the furniture and accommodation were scanty and primitive, but we were thankful for the shelter and our supper. He was very relieved when Totty and I said we much preferred beer to tea. Next morning, after being entertained with the greatest kindness and hospitality, we proceeded on our way to Neechindepur, a very tedious journey but nothing to that of the night before from the station to Mr Glassford's, as the road was completely blocked by fallen trees. My father was extremely relieved to see us as he had hardly expected that we could have started at all, but our house in Circular Road was no longer a safe abode.

Another, and rather bizarre, incident at Chuadanga station was later recounted by VHP's eldest son. [37] A Roman Catholic priest had been attacked and eaten by a tiger, whereupon the station master, with typical, bureaucratic attention to topographical accuracy, telegraphed his head-office in Calcutta; 'TIGER KILLED POPE. NO. 2 PLATFORM. WIRE INSTRUCTIONS.'

Chapter 8

The First Children and an Unexpected Inheritance

On their return to Calcutta, Lewis and VHP rented a house at No 9, Elysium Row, and it was there that their first son, christened with the same name as his father, but always known as 'Lal', was born on April 19, 1865. When 'Lal' was about six weeks old, they were invited to stay with their friends the Knowles so that VHP could recuperate after her confinement. Spring had by now turned into summer, the thermometer was registering over 100°F in the shade and the sun bore down relentlessly on those not suitably dressed.

> We went down on a Thursday I think, and the following day Lewis went up to town and came back in the evening not feeling at all well. He got frightfully ill and by 5 a.m. he had fallen unconscious in the bed with heat apoplexy. The local doctor was most kind and clever but he sent for Dr. Fane from Calcutta. They shaved Lewis's head and mustard plastered his legs but told me there was not much hope of his recovery, though if he recognised me when he came to, there was a hope for both his life and his brain. At 3 p.m. he awoke and knew who I was, and I felt God had been good and given him back to me. For a month he had to be very carefully tended and sometimes his brain wandered.
>
> So we determined to go to the Nilgiri Hills, but the question was who to take with us? The ayah was too old and the bearers could not cross the 'Kalapanis'. In my dilemma, our gigantic cook volunteered to go as nurse/ayah for 'Lal', and excellent we found him on the voyage, when we were all more or less hors-de-combat, for it was the monsoon and we had a fearful tossing.
>
> We were swung off the ship onto catamarans and pitched onto the beach at Madras. There we stayed a few days with the Egertons who had a delightful house on the sea-shore. They were awfully kind to us and made best arrangements for our journey to Coimbattore and Coonor. We went in bullock carts, where one

had to crawl in under an awning and trust that a tiger would not find you on the way. Our first night out – at Matapollium – was horrible, sleeping on a truckle bed with the wall between the rooms only halfway up, and we would watch the rats careering along the top of it wondering when they would drop onto you.

I remember my delight on reaching Coonor and putting up at Gray's Hotel, where we had a real homelike roast fowl and apple tart and cream! There was also a lovely hedge of heliotrope that delighted equally one's eyes and one's nose. Then we moved on to Silk's Hotel at Ooty, where Lewis took up riding again but all the time I was haunted by the fear that Lewis might have another relapse, because he was an obstreperous patient. Our doctor had said that he had only known of one such severe case of heat-stroke that had lived through it and that man had gone off his head. So I used to get the most appalling headaches as if my head had been split open. Lewis made me drink port wine after dinner as a tonic, which was very enjoyable, sitting in a comfortable chair by a roaring wood fire. The view of the Ghat at sunset was gorgeous, with the mists rolling along in every hue of the rainbow.

At the end of the hot season they returned to Calcutta and shared a house at 41 Chowringhee with a senior barrister in Lewis's chambers who was a bachelor. There they stayed through the cooler winter months when Lewis's services were much in demand. This meant that they could afford the return trip to the UK to spend the summer of the following year at Lewis's family home at Lovesgrove, where Veronica met her rather intimidating mother-in-law for the first time. They had brought back with them a young Indian manservant, who caused some consternation in the Welsh countryside. *The boy was allowed a gun and some cartridges to shoot rabbits in the evening. He nearly frightened the keeper out of his wits, seeing a black face with a row of white teeth grinning at him over the hedge. He thought it was the devil himself and fled away home in great terror!*

Lewis's parents were very averse to the idea of him returning to India, claiming that *a diet of potatoes and butter milk would be much better for him than curries.* So he found himself a place in some chambers in London, and the couple moved to a house in Bayswater that had been found for them, along with two other servants, by their friend Elizabeth Garrett. Lewis's brother Griffith came to lodge with them as well. He had been studying to be a doctor but had changed to reading for the bar because he did not like anatomical dissections and could see from Lewis's experience that this was potentially far more profitable. He had fallen in love with VHP's sister 'Emmy' and hoped that his revised qualifications, and Lewis's introductions, would make him instantly acceptable to James Hills as another son-in-law.

VHP was pregnant with their second child and had arranged for a mid-wife/maternity nurse to come up from Wales in due course, but matters took an unexpected turn on March 11, 1867, when the baby *arrived all of a sudden* and Lewis had to deal with the situation, assisted by Elizabeth Garrett. This was a stroke of good fortune because Elizabeth Garrett was a truly remarkable woman. In 1860, at the age of 24 and inspired by the example of Dr. Elizabeth Blackwell in America, she set out on a crusade to open the medical profession to women in Britain. She started off as a nurse at the Middlesex Hospital and recalled to VHP her earliest experiences at a maternity hospital for the poorest women. *Elizabeth frequently had the entire care of a dozen babies for whom not a scrap of clothing had been provided, so she had to beg, borrow or steal clothes for them as best she could.* She was refused admission to the medical school at the Middlesex Hospital but allowed to attend lectures provided she paid for them and her father provided the funds for these and a private tutor as well. In 1865, after more private tuition by Professors in Edinburgh and St. Andrews, she managed to obtain a licence from the Society of Apothecaries. Banned because of her sex from taking up a medical post in any hospital, she opened her own practice, first in Upper Berkeley Street, London and then as the St Mary's Dispensary for Women & Children at 69 Seymour Place. During the cholera epidemic of 1866, she treated 3,000 patients. [38]

VHP's new baby was christened Veronica Charlotte after her mother and grandmother. But almost immediately another crisis arose when the cook threatened to leave because her bedroom had become infested with bats. So the family uprooted themselves to a new address at Wallington Crescent in Paddington, with VHP and her baby being taken along with their various chattels on the back of the furniture wagon. The weather that spring was foul – VHP recorded that Lewis and Griffith went to the Derby and returned in a snow-storm. But Lewis had lost seniority in the London chambers and his case-load was less than satisfactory, *so we were determined to try India again, and if the climate did not suit him, we thought we would go to the colonies, probably Australia. I took out Veronica and left 'Lal' at Lovesgrove.*

Griffith and 18 year-old 'Emmy' sailed out to India with them, he to join Lewis in his Calcutta chambers and she to go and look after her father at Neechindepur. 'Emmy' had little self-confidence at that stage in her life, 'which gave her deep-set eyes the piteous, appealing look of a lost kitten'. She had not seen her father since she was a child and his greeting on her arrival probably did little to boost her self-esteem. 'Well, well! You're not half as ugly as they said you were!' [39]

Christmas 1867 was a thoroughly jolly family affair, with picnics and pig-sticking parties and James Hills able to make the acquaintance of his latest grand-daughter, just 9 months old. Back in Calcutta and living in a house on London Road, Lewis received a bolt from the blue on February 19th, when a telegram arrived to say that 'Uncle Pugh', his mother's bachelor brother, had died suddenly and named Lewis as his principal heir. **[Plate 25]** This was totally unexpected because Lewis was not the eldest son. He had an elder brother, John Evans who was a vicar and, by all accounts, 'unworldly in matters of property'. 'Uncle Pugh' (1810-1868) had been a banker in Aberystwyth and had himself inherited a sizeable fortune from his own father, 'Old Lewis Pugh' (1776-1850), and the story of how this had been made is of some interest as illustrating how the mineral resources of Wales, combined with luck and enterprise, could make men of modest ancestry very rich indeed.

There is evidence that this line of Pughs were descended from the Pughs of Mathervan, the area around the headwaters of the River Dovey, who could claim ancestry from a number of Welsh princes. [40] 'Old Lewis Pugh' **[Plate 24]** was the son of Humphfey Pugh (1736-1823), a builder and contractor who had been responsible for building the Town Hall in Aberystwyth and most of the bridges in Cardiganshire. 'Old Lewis Pugh' was one of his younger sons who had started his career as an apprentice saddler, but his father recognised his potential and it was to him that he left his construction business. This overruling of the principle of 'primogenita' would set a precedent.

Around 1830 'Old Lewis Pugh' was approached by a mining engineer who had been engaged by a company that was planning to exploit some lead ore resources at Cwm Ystwyth near the Devil's Bridge at the head of the Rheidol valley. The company had been forced into liquidation before the mine had been fully commissioned, but the engineer persuaded him to lease the rights from the Powell family of Nanteos and invest £500 to sink the final shaft. The earlier scheme had envisaged that the ore would be taken by packhorses to the canal at Llanidloes and thence by canal to Birmingham, but instead he built a new road along the Rheidol valley. The price of lead in 1834 was £12 per ton but it rose to a peak of £24 in 1836 before levelling out at around £17. The mines gave a lead yield of 1,294 tons in 1841, falling back to 777 tons in 1844, the year the operation was sold on. A mine promoter, Absolom Griffith, wrote that 'Pugh must have realised more than a quarter of a million pounds sterling from working the property (before outgoings and royalties)', which allowed him, among other things, to give his daughter Eliza a dowry of her weight in gold sovereigns when she married in 1830. Some of these were used to buy the 200 acre farm at Lovesgrove [see Map 2], allowing them to relocate from their smallholding near Towyn and generally move up in the world. Now that the family was self-sufficient, they also bought the neighbouring farm which was then rented out.

At his death in 1850 'Old Lewis Pugh' was worth over £100,000, which passed to his bachelor son Lewis, 'Uncle Pugh', after bequests of £4,000 to each of his Evans grandchildren. This, very wisely, was used to pay for the education of the younger boys at English public schools. In 1852 'Uncle Pugh' had bought the Abermaed estate from the Earl of Lisburne, consisting of 20 farms spread over about 1,500 acres and it was this that he now left to Lewis on his death in 1868. A codicil to his will stated that he wished him to add the additional surname of Pugh to his own, making him Lewis Pugh Evans Pugh. (This led to a further complication for family historians, quite apart from the succession of children called Lewis. Veronica was a Miss Evans, but all her younger brothers and sisters were Pughs.)

We had less than a week to get packed and the only berths available were on the Messangerie boat to Marseilles; we had a horrible journey and Veronica got whooping cough and gave it to me. The boat had started its journey in Canton and the crew were making a profitable business on the side selling chinaware, of which Lewis bought a considerable amount. Landing at Marseilles, they took the train up to Paris where VHP, on the back of Lewis's sudden good fortune, could indulge for the first time her passion for smart clothes. *I got a lovely black silk 'princess' gown and two bonnets, one a dream of tulle and wild roses. I also bought a pale green evening dress, which got deluged with soda-water at the Archery Ball.* Back in Wales, they moved into 'Uncle Pugh's' house at 21 Bridge Street, Aberystwyth, while they planned the rebuilding of Abermaed house, and it was there on Xmas Eve 1868 that their third child was born and christened with the name of Alice. But there were complications, and in spite of Elizabeth Garrett coming all the way up from London the baby died on January 17. VHP was heartbroken for months.

For the complete reconstruction and expansion of Abermaed, they were persuaded to use the services of the distinguished architect John Pollard Seddon, who was working at the same time on the University buildings and the Castle Hotel at Aberystwyth. The design for the house was in the fashionable high-Victorian Baronial style and VHP wrote later that *it was difficult to bring his ideas down to ours.* Seddon was seldom on site to organise the building work that dragged on over three years and overran the original budget by a factor of 3 times. Seddon's reputation was based on building churches and municipal buildings and this was his first private house; he made a complete mess of the internal drainage, which had to be completely rebuilt. Lewis was anxious to include an ice-house in the cellars, but his grandson later claimed that this never worked and only added to the drainage problems. A large conservatory, or winter-garden, was added on one side which VHP later filled with exotic plants from all over the world, and internally there was purpose-built furniture to Seddon's designs while the wallpapers were commissioned from the workshops of William Morris. With its steeply pitched roofs, multi-coloured stonework and high-ceilinged rooms, the final result is not appealing to modern taste, though Veronica claimed that it was *a very beautiful building and many came to see it and admire it.* [41] **[Plate 26]**

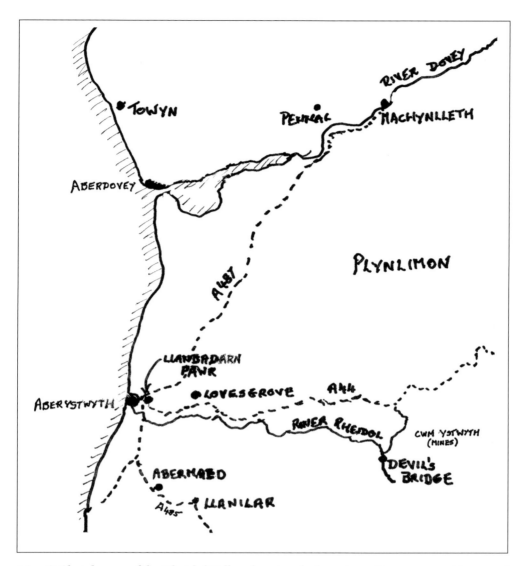

Map 2. Sketch map of the Rheidol Valley showing the location of Lovesgrove, Abermaed and Pennal in relation to Aberystwyth.

While the house was being constructed, Lewis had a walled garden built that contained potting sheds two-stories high; according to his son, the high walls were a yard thick, though this may have been youthful exaggeration. And he bought more land from the Pryces of Gogerddan, extending the estate by over 4,000 acres of moorland on the slopes of Plynlimon. All this extravagant expenditure began to stretch the family finances. Added to which, Lewis was finding life difficult at the London bar with not enough work coming in, and although the Conservative association asked him to let them nominate him as a candidate for the next election, *they were too 'stuck in the mud' altogether for him and he declined.* They spent the winters up in London renting a house in Devonshire Street where their next child, James 'Jimmy' Pugh, was born in January 1870. (He grew up to be rather a tearaway and was killed in a bizarre shooting incident in Calcutta at the age of 25, as recounted later.)

> *On December 2, 1871, our third son 'Archy' was born. Just before that, Jimmy got scarlet fever and I was packed off to London; dear Totty was with me and Lewis came up just in time to welcome our new arrival. When 'Archy' was about six weeks, I went for a drive in an open Victoria, caught a chill on my breasts and was dreadfully ill with ulcers on both of them. So Archy had to be weaned and brought up on a bottle; the only one of my children who was in fact the biggest and sturdiest of them all! He never had an ache or a pain and never caught any infectious disease.*

November the following year saw the birth of their next child, a little girl christened Ellinor though always known as 'Nellie'. And it was just after this event that James Hills returned from India for what would prove to be the last time.

Chapter 9

The Death of James Hills

The road from Neechindepur to the railway station was lined by all the villagers, his 'children', completely unaware that they would never see James Hills' weather-beaten, be-whiskered face again. **[Plate 10]** Perhaps he himself faced up to the reality of the situation because he drew up his will before he departed. [42] Arriving in London, he was able to catch up with several members of his family. Lewis and VHP were renting a house in Dorset Square and 'Totty' Cubitt and her children were staying with them while her husband was serving on the North West frontier, alongside her brother Colonel 'Jimmy' Hills VC who had just distinguished himself in the Lushai campaign. James Hills' eldest son Archibald, who had sold his indigo operation for practically nothing, was living with his wife nearby, though when he went down with erysipelas – painful lesions on the face – she went to live on her own *and left him to his fate*, which cemented VHP's opinion of her. 'Emmy', now 24, moved in to nurse him and cook for him.

George, James Hills' fourth son and *the quietest but the most amusing*, had retired from the Royal Engineers in India after losing an eye playing racquets and was living in lodgings on Dover Street and it was with him that his father went to stay. In her memoirs, VHP recalled her brother with affection.

> *He was a regular old bachelor and quite a lady's man, but unfortunately he was apt to choose his visits in the childrens' holidays so was rather in their way and he in ours. When the children were all unusually riotous, he used to say he found he had a great sympathy and fellow feeling for King Herod in the massacre of the innocents! Really, he was the kindest old soul possible and nearly as clever as Ernest Ormond at getting extra leave.* [43] *For a long time he had the appointment as executive engineer in Assam and made the beautiful road to Shilling. He wanted to make a drive through Abermaed, but as the cost would have come out of our pocket and not the Government's we declined.*

James Hills was now aged 71 and had lived nearly all his life in Bengal, through the windy winters, the torrential monsoons and the parching, dusty days of high summer. He had never spared himself physically, while emotionally he had never really got over the tragic loss of his young wife through 22 years of widowhood. He had known two periods of great wealth but also two strokes of financial misfortune and now Elliot Macnaughton had told him that he must foreclose the mortgage on Neechindepur. So his main object in returning to England had been to raise new funds and to this end he wished to arrange an urgent meeting with James Mackenzie, his one-time assistant, who had gone on to make a fortune in indigo and became one of the main money-lenders to Edward Prince of Wales, helping to finance the lavish life-style that Queen Victoria disapproved of so much. (His reward would be an elevation to the peerage, as the 1st Baronet Mackenzie of Glen Muick in 1890.) Mackenzie lived in a grand mansion near Marble Arch where VHP and 'Emmy' had been frequent visitors, on one occasion witnessing the reception for Princess Alexandra three days before her wedding to Edward, Prince of Wales.

December 13, 1872, was a bitterly cold day, with icy winds blowing along Oxford Street and Mackenzie kept James Hills waiting for several hours before he finally came out to say that there was nothing he could do for him. Chilled to the bone and with his hopes dashed, he trudged back through Mayfair to the lodgings in Dover Street.

That afternoon 'Emmy' came round to VHP's house utterly exhausted from nursing her brother Archibald and begged to stay the night. *It was all too much for her and she was like a parched pea, poor darling. We feared she had the rheumatic fever for she ached so much all over, but it was just nerves and exhaustion, for she never would take care of herself or spare herself in any way.* There was no spare bed for her at Dorset Square *but a bed was made up in the study downstairs and Nurse Gibson took her in charge.* Griffith Evans had come up from Wales earlier in the day before catching a boat that evening to return to Calcutta.

He came to see me with a most lovely bunch of flowers. After chatting a while, he got up to go and I asked him if he would not like to see Emmy before he went. He looked surprised and asked if I thought Emmy would like to see him, and I said I was sure she would. So he went down and chatted about indifferent matters till he said goodbye and was at the door, when she cried out 'Griffith I want you!' So back he came and 'it' was settled – after nine years waiting for her and many askings, but her reply had always been 'I like you better than anyone but daddy', which he had always found discouraging. He was eager to go round and see our father at once, before he set sail, but Emmy begged him not to as she wished to do so herself when she saw him the next day. He had always been so anxious for it, as we all had been; but that telling never came.

The following morning James Hills was brought breakfast by his landlady, Mrs Bennett.

She was a very sweet woman and wonderfully like my mother. He said he felt rather tired, so she persuaded him to rest on the couch and helped him to lie down, and he just gave a sigh and was gone.

Lewis had gone to enquire after Archibald and came back to break the news to me, which he did so tenderly and lovingly, for he had a great affection for my father. Dear Emmy was very anxious to come up and tell me about the great event of the day before and Mrs Gibson went to help her dress and persuaded her to put on her black dress – in those days it was quite the fashion to have a black frock, a sort of 'go-anywhere-outfit' when one did not know what one was expected to wear. 'But I want to have a bit of blue ribbon round my neck to brighten it up' said Emmy, and then Lewis went and told her of our father's death. Poor child, he had been all the world to her! Lewis carried her upstairs and laid her on the bed beside me. My poor darling, she was so distressed that she had not allowed Griffith to tell him about their engagement, for she knew how glad he would have been.

James Hills was buried in a vault in Kensal Green cemetery, north London, beside a small mausoleum to the Dukes of Cambridge. [44] 'Sacred to the memory of James Hills Esq. of Neechindepur, Kishnagur, Bengal, who died suddenly in London on 14.12.1872 aged 71. This monument is erected by his family in grateful memory of a father much beloved by them and respected by all who knew him. Peace be with him.' A memorial slab was also erected in the graveyard of the mission church at Neechindepur, alongside that of the wife he had adored. In his memoirs, Sir Henry Cotton, who was appointed as the magistrate for the district of Chuadanga soon after he joined the Indian Civil Service in 1867, gives a fulsome pen-portrait of him, which contrasts markedly from his views on some other English landlords. Cotton was a sympathiser with those of both nationalities who wished to see a reasoned and rational progression towards greater Indian integration and self-rule, becoming one of the few non-Indians on the Indian National Congress and its chairman in 1904.

'The Prince of indigo planters in the 19th century was James Hills. His power in my time was practically unlimited and it was ever exercised for good. The tenants of the estate looked with an extraordinary and almost idolatrous reverence upon their *burra sahib*; "During the inundation, did not Mr Hills, at a cost of one lakh of rupees, get rice from the East and seed for our cold-weather crops and support us into another year?" In later days, when circumstances had gone hard for his concerns, I have known the headmen of some of the interested villages to club together and declare that they would sell everything they had rather than pay their rents to another landlord.

This time-honoured old Scottish gentleman was as esteemed and trusted by the officials of the Government as he was respected by his people. His sterling benevolence and good sense had marked him through successive administrations as an exceptional member of a class in which so favourable an exception was all too uncommon. His generous hospitality, his frank and open deportment, his ready acceptance of the European traveller, his irreproachable courtesy, his kindness to the country-folk, who would daily flock to ask his advice or aid, had endeared him to all who knew him.' [45]

VHP recalled her father's passing with loving but stoical realism.

On reflection, we felt it was perhaps the best thing that could have happened to him. The glory had departed and left him old and impoverished. He, who had been a prince over much land, now had none to call his own, and his home, which had always been open to all, had passed on to those who had become enriched at his expense. Thus he ended his life in a London lodging, loved and honoured to the last. A wonderful career – cast by the waves onto the shores of India in his shirt – half a century of great prosperity, then all gone and he returned to this country as poor as he started. While he lived, he was like a watered garden and a blessing to all around him, and he was spared the evil of a broken down old age.

Chapter 10

A Member of Parliament, Marriages and Murder

When James Hills died, he had ten surviving children and twenty two grandchildren already, with many more to follow later. Many of these would lead interesting, and in some cases extraordinary, lives but space prevents a wide-ranging account of them all. What follows is restricted to those who continued to have strong ties with India, and an interest in indigo in particularly. One family will be followed for the next three generations and the link to the other great Indian export – opium. Summaries of the careers of James Hills' sons who remained in India will follow later in another chapter but for now we will take up the threads of the two daughters who married the two Welsh brothers.

'Emmy' and Griffith Evans were married on September 4, 1873, at the church of St Hilary in Llanilar **[Plate 27]** with Veronica as one of seven bridesmaids, and that evening Lewis and VHP staged a magnificent fancy-dress ball at Abermaed. The house was still not completely finished. Nothing like it had ever been seen in the neighbourhood, the champagne flowed and the dancing went on until 4 o'clock in the morning, with VHP dressed as Berengaria. *I had my hair down and a purple velvet gown with a green satin front and a crown and a long tulle veil. Our house was packed full, and something went wrong with the plumbing, so the hot water in the baths was all rusty and Lewis's hair was dyed a reddish brown! The following morning for breakfast the guests had to scrounge what they could from the leftovers of the night before, and the only thing to drink was Worcester sauce.*

Very soon after their honeymoon, 'Emmy' and Griffith, Lewis and VHP and their baby 'Nellie' all set off for India again. The trip was now much quicker; express trains across Europe, steam-ships rather than sail, and passage through the Suez Canal. But only a few weeks after their arrival in Calcutta, a telegram arrived to say that Elizabeth, sister of the two brothers and married to a clergyman Howell Edwards, had died of a hernia in her late 30s, leaving her much older husband with three teenage children. This must have been a shattering blow to the Evans parents because the next telegram stated that they had both died within ten days of each other. Furthermore, Lewis's agent and estate manager at Abermaed, Mr. Charles Williams, had also died, so it was agreed that Lewis and VHP would return home at once to sort matters out.

> *We came via Brindisi and made the night journey to Naples. It was lovely in the early morning, and as we drove to our hotel we were run after by boys selling flowers, and Lewis bought a huge bouquet of white lilac and heliotrope, which reminded us of our days in the hills. We hurried up to our rooms and demanded a bath, much to the amusement of the manager, but he eventually managed to produce one on wheels, which we pushed into our room, followed by a small army of men with buckets and barrels of hot water and towels.*

Baby 'Nellie' had now spent most of her life so far at sea, just like her elder sister Veronica, and VHP herself was pregnant again. She gave birth to a baby boy on July 9, 1874, and he was christened Herbert Owain Pugh, *the first name after Herbert Knowles, our old Indian friend who had been so good to us in 1865 when Lewis nearly died in his house at Tatighur, and Owain after an ancestor who had been a famous Welsh judge.* The christening took place in the church at Llanbadarn Fahr, which was in the middle of the farms on the Abermaed estate. Rebuilding the east end of the church soon became one of many projects Lewis now undertook, along with a complete reconstruction of the home farm at Tanygraig, with the results *inspiring the admiration of the neighbourhood.* While VHP concentrated on planting up the new gardens with the help of their immensely tall and aged Scottish gardener, Hutchinson, Lewis extended the woodlands, planting several thousand new trees and employing six woodsmen.

VHP's seventh (surviving) child was born the following year on November 16 and baptised as Evelyn Anne Pugh. (When she grew up, she married into the Sellar family and, as we will see later, became the catalyst for another wedding that forged the link between the two parts of this book.) The birth of Evelyn was supposed to coincide with 'Emmy' and Griffith's second baby – the first had only survived a few hours – but Alice Evans arrived two months prematurely as they were on board ship returning to England. With the baby *wrapped in cotton wool surrounded by hot-water bottles and looking like a scrawny chicken,* the two families managed to arrive safely at Abermaed. The Evans' old family home of Lovesgrove had been left to the brothers' maiden sister Mary Margaret Evans and now Griffith agreed to buy it off her and start planning a completely new, larger house higher up the slope behind. This would finally be completed in 1882 as a comfortable, unostentatious country house with quite low ceilings, in complete contrast to the wildly extravagant Abermaed. VHP gave birth to another child in December 1878, Roland Anthony Corderan Pugh, while 'Emmy' followed suit a couple of months later, a son who was christened Griffith after his father.

Lewis was appointed as a Justice of the Peace in 1879 and a Deputy Lord Lieutenant for the county of Cardigan, and had the great honour of presiding over the Eistedfford on New Year's Day 1880. Then – yet more expenses – he was adopted as the Liberal candidate to contest the Cardigan County Parliamentary seat at Westminster in the General Election that spring. For three weeks, Lewis and VHP were involved in hectic canvassing while Griffith and 'Emmy' managed the campaign headquarters from lodgings they took in the Terrace at Aberystwyth.

We canvassed the whole county from Eglwysfach in the north to Cardigan in the south, mostly in Lewis's Perth dogcart with a pair of horses. Everywhere we were received with enthusiasm – people of the villages came out to greet us and in many places the horses were taken out of the carriage and we were drawn into the meeting place by our supporters. We had the most perfect days of sunshine and we must have covered over 700 miles. But Lewis was opposed by nearly all the gentry in the county – in the north the Pryces and the Waddinghams of Hafod were about the only ones who supported us. The rest of the gentry were all jealous of Lewis's talent, his gift of speech in both English and Welsh, and his good-looks. One paper described him as 'the Adonis of the party'. On the other hand, our opponent – the sitting member, a Mr Lloyd of Llangoedmore – was a feeble man.

The final result was a resounding victory by 801 votes; Lewis and VHP were greeted in Aberystwyth *by a crowd so densely packed that you could have walked along their heads.* VHP's memoirs about special occasions tended to concentrate on two things – her cascades of auburn hair, of which she was justly proud, and the clothes that she wore.

Of course I had to have a special frock for the occasion which was made up by Mrs Lewis. It was a dark blue material with a light blue fringed top and went with a toque in navy-blue silk covered with forget-me-nots. A lady told me more than 30 years later that she remembered our driving round the town, my hair and my blue bonnet and that it set the fashion in Aberystwyth for the year.

After the election, they went up to London for the season, to attend political functions and the 'levee' at Buckingham Palace where VHP was presented to Queen Victoria. *It was all a beautiful sight. My dress was lovely; the train was of olive green duchesse satin trimmed with bunches of water lilies and the front and skirt were a pale sea-green satin. Dear 'Totty' lent me our mother's emeralds and 'Lizzie' her pearls and the diamond cross.* **[Plate 23]**

Lewis made his maiden speech, on the supply of ordnance to the army, to the House of Commons on June 4. There had been disturbing news from Afghanistan early in the year with the fighting around Kabul, though VHP recorded her delight when her brother 'Jimmy' Hills VC had been promoted to Major-General and given command of a Division. On July 29, she noted news of *General Burrow's disaster and the retreat to Kandahar; also the shooting of General Brooke on Aug 16.* But the arrival of General 'Bobs' Roberts, to support his old friend 'Jimmy', resulted in the victory that she could note on Sept 3, and the whole family was at Charing Cross on November 13 to greet the returning heroes. Four weeks later, VHP's last child, Marjorie, was born on December 10. [46]

In the autumn of 1881 both families decided to return to India, leaving London by train on October 29. VHP took her new baby, plus a nanny and a maid. They endured a very rough crossing to Calais, followed by a succession of trains to a dawn arrival at Brindisi on the 31st, followed by an even rougher crossing of the Mediterranean to Alexandria. *Everyone seasick; furniture and everything tumbling about. I had to change baby after breakfast and then make nurse and Martha get up, which makes them feel better.* Rather than travel down the Suez Canal, they all took the overnight sleeper to Zagazey and boarded their ship for the final stage via Aden (November 10), reaching Bombay on the 15th *where there was frightful confusion.* After an overnight stay in Watson's Hotel and a morning's sightseeing, they caught the evening train to Calcutta which they reached at 6 am on the 19th and were met by VHP's dapper, bachelor brother 'Charlie', a partner in the indigo-brokers Thomas & Co.

The whole journey had taken three weeks and is quoted in some detail to show the impact of changes to transport had that had occurred since VHP's first trip back to England exactly 30 years earlier, one that had lasted over six months. Speed had been achieved at the expense of some considerable inconvenience; frequent changes from one mode to another, brief overnight stays in hotels, timing connections and, a nightmare for the men in the party, organising porters for all the luggage and the general paraphernalia of travelling with a baby and staff. At least there were some little luxuries and VHP noted with relief that their lunch boxes on the Calcutta Mail train were accompanied by small hampers *that contained ice and soda water, claret and brandy.*

After spending Christmas in Delhi and Agra, they were back in Calcutta for the fancy-dress ball given by the Viceroy, Lord Ripon, on January 11, where the two sisters caused quite a stir. 'Emmy' went as a witch while VHP was the 'old woman who lived in a shoe' with baby Marjorie in her arms. She paid a brief two-day visit back to Neechindepur at the beginning of February, mainly to tend her mother's grave and see that her father's memorial slab has been built according to plan. Lewis and VHP then headed home again, arriving at Victoria late in the evening of March 26. He attended to constituency business and was back in London for the opening of Parliament on April 17. VHP joined him up in London by May 17 for Mrs Gladstone's 'At Home', only to find it had to be postponed *on account of the murders in Dublin*. On May 27 she went to the Lyceum theatre with her sister 'Lizzie' and her husband to see 'Romeo & Juliet', which she was delighted with *in spite of Henry Irving's ugliness*.

The major event in the summer of 1882 was the marriage of her brother Major-General Sir 'Jimmy' Hills VC. His last command had been the 3rd Division of the Northern Afghanistan Field Force and on his retirement he was awarded KCB for his services, along with a vote of thanks by both Houses of Parliament the previous May. He was now 49 and his bride, Elizabeth 'Betha' Johnes, was only two years younger. **[Plates 38 & 39]** She was the second daughter of Judge Johnes of Dolaucothi in Cardiganshire, who, on the morning of August 19, 1876, had dismissed his butler, an Irishman by the name of Henry Tremble, for drunkenness. Tremble had immediately got hold of a gun, murdered Judge Johnes and then severely wounded his widowed daughter, Mrs Cookson, before shooting all the dogs and finally turning the gun on himself. 'Betha' Johnes, now the heiress, had fortunately been away on a visit.

The impact of this tragic incident on the Welsh people was summarised in '*The Welshman*' newspaper of August 22. 'This wise and just and good man, so honoured, so beloved by all who knew him, died as he had lived, preserving even in the bitterness of his death his characteristic of calm resignation. He died commending his soul to his maker and breathing out words of blessing on his children. At the Wrexham Eisteddford on the 22nd of August, the Bishop and the whole assembly stood up and simultaneously uncovered in solemn silence – a scene never to be forgotten in the annals of Wales.' The couple were married in Westminster Abbey on September 15, 1882 with Veronica as a bridesmaid again, after which he adopted the surname of Hills-Johnes, the name under which he is recorded in the annals of the Victoria Cross. And the following day 'Emmy' gave birth to a daughter, christened Betha Evans in honour of her new aunt.

Chapter 11

A Political Storm and a Colliery Disaster

Lewis returned to Calcutta for the winter sessions on November 2 and wrote home with delight to say that he had been given briefs and retainers worth Rupees 2,000 within a couple of days of his arrival. He returned to England for the opening of Parliament the following April and spoke in support of the Affirmation Bill, allowing witnesses to 'Affirm' their statements rather than 'swearing an oath' on the Bible, which caused considerable offence in certain quarters of the Welsh press. But a much greater political storm was brewing, one that would thrust Lewis onto the horns of a dilemma and make him question where his true loyalty should lie; to his family and his father-in-law's memory or the Prime Minister of the political party of which he was now a representative. Lewis was anxious to return to Calcutta in October, just as the Liberals were introducing a highly contentious Bill into Parliament – and the 'whips' were out.

The origins of this controversial piece of legislation went back to 1880 when Lord Ripon was appointed Viceroy of India. He had set about introducing liberal measures that were in tune with Gladstone's political philosophy in Britain, reducing the salt tax and removing protective duties while encouraging progressive developments in both primary and secondary education. But when he tried to introduce an amendment to the legislation that would extend the right of Indian judges and magistrates to try cases involving European defendants into rural districts, he ran into a storm of protest, mainly from the owners of tea and indigo plantations in Bengal but also from English women living in India. This, the Indian Criminal Procedure Bill, was more commonly known as the Ilbert Bill after the man who had recently been appointed as the legal advisor to the Council of India. It also stirred up vociferous opposition back in England, particularly from the Tory benches in Parliament and the Anglo-Indian Association. The editor of *The Times* was bombarded by angry letter-writers. A packed rally was held in the St. James Hall on

June 24, 1883, under the chairmanship of Sir Alexander Arbuthnot, lately a member of the Supreme Council of India, which concluded with the setting up of an 'action committee', including Mr Melville Macnaughton, son of James Hills' erstwhile friend Elliot Macnaughton and now the owner of Neechindepur. Leading the opposition on behalf of the Bar Association in Calcutta was Griffith Evans.

On the day before Lewis was due to return to India, he received a telegram summoning him to the offices of Lord Grosvenor at 10 Downing Street the following morning, a meeting he decided not to attend. Instead he wrote a letter to Lord Winchester, the chief whip, explaining his position and caught the boat-train for Dover on the evening of October 26. This action threw the future of his political career into jeopardy. Arriving in Calcutta, he worked with his brother Griffith on an amendment to the Ilbert Bill that finally allowed it to be passed in both legislatures, whereby white people appearing before an Indian magistrate could demand trial by a jury in which there had to be a minimum of six non-Indians. This 'emasculation' of the Bill became the major catalyst leading to the formation of the Indian National Congress, which in turn became the dominant factor in Indian politics for the next seventy years. Lord Dufferin, the Viceroy from 1884 to 1888, recognised the significance of the formation of the Indian National Congress following the Ilbert Bill and 'gave it a remote and olympian blessing'. [47] Even in its early days, the one group who would not partake in the Congress were the Muslims; Sir Sayid Ahmed Khan pronounced, prophetically, that 'democratic government would be government by Hindus'.

In December, the London newspapers were reporting, erroneously, that Lewis had accepted a Judgeship in India, leading to a letter from his agent, Col. Pryce, to VHP demanding to know the truth. *Very worrying time, constant telegrams about Lewis's resignation,* but in spite of her pleas for him to return, Lewis wrote that he was not intending to come back until the spring.

These matters were not VHP's only worries in January 1884. The extravagant expenditure on Abermaed combined with a farming recession had put a damaging strain on their finances and Lewis had been persuaded, in order to provide what was assumed to be a secure dividend, to invest £10,000 for a minority shareholding in a colliery in South Wales. This, the Garnant Colliery Company, was owned primarily by his parliamentary colleague David Pugh (no relation), the MP for Carmarthenshire. In 1874 the company had opened an anthracite-coal mine in the Amman valley which lies about 12 miles north of Swansea in the foothills of the Black Mountains. It was known as 'Pwll Perkins' and employed 150 miners.

On the morning of Wednesday, January 16 1884 an accident occurred when the cage was being lowered down the shaft and the wire rope snapped, the miners on board, including four boys, being killed instantly when the cage hit the bottom of the shaft 225ft below. An enquiry concluded that the cage had been overloaded – 10 miners instead of the mandatory 8 – but that this was not the cause of the accident. Nor was the integrity of the wire rope, which had only recently been renewed, put into question. What seemed to have happened was that the door of the cage had partially opened during the early stages of the descent, temporarily snagging the cage against its guide rails and causing a slack to develop in the cable. The cage had then freed itself, possibly by the miners rocking the sides, and the sudden snatch when the slack was taken up overloaded the rope beyond its tensile strength. A magistrate's court decided that the brakeman was responsible for the accident, perhaps for letting the cage down too fast, and he was initially charged with manslaughter. But after a plea from his defence lawyer this was changed to the lesser offense of lack of attention to duty and he was fined £13.00.

No question was ever raised about any responsibility on behalf of the mine company itself, which is perhaps an ironic side-note because David Pugh had been the MP who had championed the passing of the Employer's Liability Act through Parliament a few years earlier. Some local press wrongly reported that the owner was 'Mr Pugh, the MP for Cardiganshire', so VHP and her brother Sir 'Jimmy' Hills-Johnes visited the colliery on February 7 to console the relatives of the miners that had been killed, a meeting which she described in her diary as *very painful – very much distressed.*

Chapter 12

The Next Generation, a Mysterious Death and Tying Up Some Loose Ends

When Lewis finally arrived back home on April 21, 1884, he went straight to the House of Commons to discuss his future with the Liberal Party managers, but on June 4 the decision was taken that he would apply for the 'Chiltern Hundreds'. His letter of resignation was actually posted to his agent but Lord Kensington persuaded him to stay on until after October 31. Veronica, now 17, was taken to her first 'low dress' party at the end of June, *she looked so sweet and pretty*, and to a ball at Devonshire House, followed by a presentation to Mrs Gladstone, where VHP had to explain to the 'Grand Old Man' why Lewis was absent.

Lewis's last political act was to make a speech to a packed Liberal rally in Aberaeron in September, which was *greeted with great enthusiasm*. Before Lewis set off for India again on November he sold the farm at Craigwen to Mr David Howell for £4,800 and entered 'Lal' for Lincoln's Inn.[48] Other smaller farms were also disposed of, mostly to the sitting tenants though one was bought by the Bishop. The family finances were showing considerable strain.

Over the next six years their lives settled into a fairly regular pattern, with Lewis spending the majority of the year in India, returning to Wales for a month's leave in the autumn, and VHP going out to join him for a few months in the spring, accompanied by various of her children. Griffith and 'Emmy' were more permanently based in Calcutta where he was making a considerable fortune at the bar; he had also been appointed as the senior legal officer on the Viceroy's Legislative Council. They lived in an imposing house on Theatre Road, the status equivalent of Park Lane in London. Knighted for his services in 1892, he turned down the appointment to Attorney General in 1899 and returned home to Lovesgrove. **[Plates 40 & 41]**

VHP's day by day diaries give a fascinating record of life in the last decade of the 19th century, recording births, marriages, illnesses and deaths among family and friends, as well as notes on exceptional weather; floods and snow in Wales, earthquakes in India. The entries for her numerous voyages become briefer, concentrating on storms and seasickness. In Calcutta, dinner parties, dances and balls at Government House figure prominently, along with VHP's charitable work at orphanages, a dispensary and women's workgroups. She and Lewis took trips to Simla and Darjeeling (where VHP was 'trollied' down the railway which she found very exciting), Agra and Barrackpore, sometimes staying as the guests of the local Maharajah when they are also Lewis's clients. From Wales, the entries are about church fetes and tennis parties, playing the harmonica for church services and detailed domestic accounts including staff wages, which on one occasion had to be cut. When 'Emmy' was at Lovesgrove the sisters spent much time in each other's company as the younger of the two produced a succession of healthy children over the years – a total of seven in all.

The colliery remained a problem. At some stage the directors wrote to Lewis to say that the operation was unprofitable and that they were planning to close it down, but somehow he managed to find the money to keep it in operation. His son wrote later; 'chasing a loss, he took over the mine and ruined himself, having got caught in a slump when the coal could not be sold for the cost of raising it. He was presented with a testimonial by his workmen for keeping the colliery open, but that was all he got.' [49] How had he raised the funds to do this? His income from legal fees enabled him to send regular payments back to VHP for the household bills at Abermaed but he had no capital left. The answer was that he mortgaged Abermaed twice, the second time to his brother Griffith for £20,000, a loan that was never repaid during his lifetime. [50]

By 1890, Veronica was 22 years old and very athletic, being particularly good at tennis, and she was with her parents in Calcutta that year when she met her future husband. **[Plate 34]** VHP's diary notes for this period have unfortunately been lost so we do not know precisely how and where they met, but it seems most likely that it was at some sporting event. John Frederick, 'Jack', Macnair was a partner in the Calcutta trading house of Begg, Dunlop and Co., a firm that specialised in the export of indigo, coffee and tea with branches in London and Cawnpore. **[Plate 35]** He was a fine polo player and pig-sticker though his best sport was golf, which he played off a scratch handicap, winning the club championship at the Calcutta Golf Club in 1885 and 1887. [51] He was the younger son of James Macnair (1796-1865), a gentleman farmer who owned an estate of 2,340 acres at Auchinech on the banks of Loch Lomond in Ayrshire. **[Plate 45]** James Macnair had overcome the handicap of going completely deaf as a teenager, due to mastoids, marrying the 18 year old

Janet Ranken in 1828 and raising a family of six children of whom 'Jack' was the second youngest. In his silent world, James Macnair became a successful yachtsman, credited with building the first metal-hulled racing yacht in which he won the regatta trophy at Oban in August 1838. [52]

'Jack' Macnair had been born in 1846 and so was 21 years older than Veronica and he was also the commanding officer of the Calcutta Light Horse Regiment. This, like the Yeomanry Regiments in the British Territorial Army, was a volunteer force of militiamen officered by gentlemen who could provide their own horses and who were prepared to give up a certain amount of their time to military training, including a fortnight's camp every year. The regiment had originally been founded as the Calcutta Volunteer Cavalry in 1759, reconstituted under various titles over the years and finally adopting the title of the Calcutta Light Horse Regiment in 1889. [53] It was while 'Jack' Macnair was back in London on business in October 1891 and Veronica was with her parents at Abermaed that they became officially engaged. 'Jack' wrote to his fiancée from his sister Anne Macfarlan's home in Wimbledon on the 16th.

> 'My beloved, what joy it was to receive your letter this morning and doubly
> so to know that you are happy and resting, but you were cruel to keep me so
> long in suspense and I had begun to think I should fail to win the love I so
> greatly prized..........Your devoted Jack'

Letters of congratulation flooded in from friends and relatives across two continents and Veronica kept every one of them; they make a fascinating archive. [54] Her uncle Sir 'Jimmy' Hills-Johnes VC wrote from Dolaucothi; 'Ever so many and warm congratulations on the happy result of Mr Macnair's visit. Knowing something of him through his relatives and also by personal contact I am really very happy that you and he have settled to run the race of life together. ... Mr Macnair is, we all think, a right good fellow and a fortunate man in having won your affection.' 'Jack's' sister Anne wrote to say that 'no one is more fitted to be a good husband than he; we have grown up from the nursery together and I have never heard him say an unkind word or even seen a cross look on his dear old face.' Certainly his droopy moustache and his active lifestyle in India made him look older than his true age of 45, and as fate would have it he did not make old bones.

The wedding was arranged hastily for November the 4th and two days later the *Cambrian News and Welsh Farmer's Gazette* devoted two whole broadsheet columns to the magnificent affair. The paper recalled Lewis Pugh's brief but active political career and how he had 'spoken up on many an occasion in the interests of the people ....Mrs Pugh also, by her acts of charity and her intelligent interests in the welfare of her neighbours has won the esteem of all and the affection of many.' The service was conducted by Lewis's younger brother, Rev. David Pugh, and there were ten bridesmaids, 'who wore dresses of white cloth trimmed with green velvet, gold and pink embroidery, with green Vandyke hats trimmed with ostrich feathers. The event was favoured not only with bright sunshine and cloudless skies but was more than usually brilliant both in the number of guests and the beauty of the costumes worn. ...... Perhaps the family would have liked to celebrate the ceremony without the intrusion of the large number of the general public which assembled from all points of the compass ..... at Llanilar Church, the assembly must have numbered close upon a thousand people and the square between the church and the Falcon was crowded with conveyances.'

Then the newspaper listed all the invited guests and detailed every single present that the bridal pair had been given, jewellery from close family members and items of silverware from practically everyone else. The staff and workmen on the Abermaed estate had clubbed together to buy a large silver punchbowl. In the days before wedding present lists, there were inevitably extensive duplications, with four sets of silver table-napkin rings and no less than six silver tea sets. The Macnair relations tended to give practical items like rugs and blankets. General Sir John Hills, VHP's brother, gave 'a pair of 5th century Peking jars from the Royal Palace of Mandalay' (probably looted during his campaign during the Burma War of 1887), while Jane Owen and Mrs Jones each gave a dozen hen's eggs.

The couple spent a very brief honeymoon at Borth, having politely declined uncle 'Bobbie' Hills' invitation to spend the time on his grouse-moor in Scotland because of the distance involved. Later VHP wrote the following pen-portrait of her short, stocky brother.

My brother Bobbie had made a pile in Calcutta and returned in 1876, taking a lovely place on the shores of Loch Rannoch near the Pass of Glencoe. He used to come and stay at Abermaed to shoot pheasants. He was much non-plussed by them – being such big birds (compared to grouse) he said you could hardly fail to miss them, but he found them very trying for all that. He was always most kind and good to our children, who went on to enjoy his hospitality at Westerton, Keith Hall and other shoots. Roland was his godson and he promised him a kilt but he never got it. For many years he remained a bachelor and did not marry until he was 59 – the very tall Miss Leonora Hay, cousin of Evelyn Fergusson, with whom she was brought up and who married Bobbie's nephew Archie Chalmers. They then proceeded to have eight children over the next ten years.

On November 12, Lewis and VHP, accompanied by their daughter 'Nellie' and son Herbert, were heading back to India on the SS *Chusan*. Writing to her daughter

Plate 1. Captain Alexander Scott, uncle of James Hills and commander of the 'Lady Lushington'.

Plate 2. The children of Archibald Hills, with James Hills top centre.

Plate 3. Dr. John Angelo Savi (1765-1831).

Plate 4. Elizabeth Corderan (1775-1859), daughter of General Andre Corderan and later the wife of Dr. Savi.

Plate 5. An imaginative reconstruction of how James Hills arrived in India following the shipwreck of August 9, 1821.

Plate 6. Two members of the Dent family purchasing land in Bengal from a zimindar circa 1780. This painting by Arthur Devis also shows the house they built subsequently and echoes the purchase of Neechindepur by James Hills.

Plate 7. Indigo factory in Bengal.

Plate 8. Indigo fermentation tanks showing the aeration process.

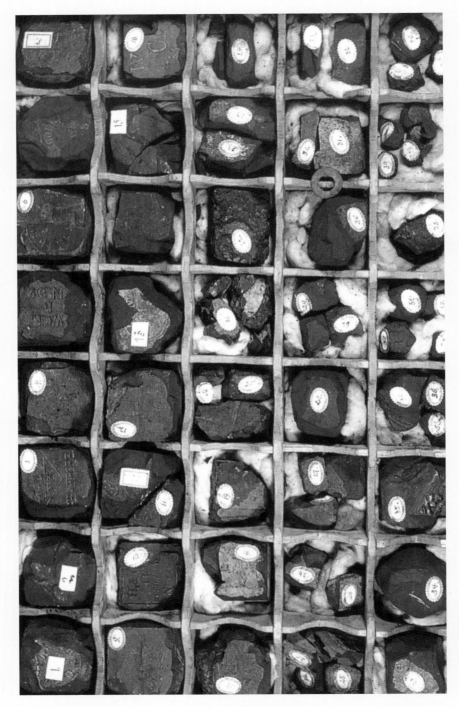

Plate 9. Museum collection with samples of different types and grades of indigo.

Plate 10. James Hills of Neechindepur (1801-1872).

Plate 11. Charlotte Savi (1813-1850), the most ravishing of the beautiful Savi daughters. Portrait painted on her engagement to James Hills in 1831.

Plate 12. Neechindepur, 'the house without anxiety', in its prime. Inset. Neechindepur in the 1970s.

Plate 13. The children of James Hills painted just after the death of his wife. The Scottish artist has imagined this composition as if they were all at Neechindepur. VHP is third from the left.

Plate 14. VHP and her brother encountering the train that had been blown over in the great cyclone of 1864. The details of the Eastern Bengal Railway locomotive are accurate, even if the scene is imagined.

Plate 15. Lt. 'Jimmy' Hills (1833-1919) – back right – with brother officers, including (centre) his lifelong friend 'Bobs' Roberts, later Lord Roberts of Khandahar VC.

Plate 16. Major 'Jimmy' Hills VC on his posting to Afghanistan, with his medals from the Indian Mutiny and the Abyssinian Campaigns.

Plate 17. Lt. 'Jimmy' Hills winning the VC at Delhi, July 9, 1857.

Plate 18. 'Totty' Hills (1840-1916), later the wife of Capt. William Cubitt VC.

Plate 19. Lt. William Cubitt (1835-1903) winning his VC on the retreat from Chinhut, Lucknow, 1857.

Plate 20. 'Lizzie' Hills (1838-1897), later the wife of Capt. Jenkin Jones RE.

Plate 21. Veronica Harriet Hills [VHP] (1844-1931).

Plate 22. Lewis Evans (later Evans-Pugh, 1837-1908), husband of VHP. Barrister, JP, MP, DL and member of the Viceroy's Advisory Council in Calcutta.

Plate 23. VHP in Court Dress for her presentation to Queen Victoria, 1880.

Plate 24. 'Old Lewis' Pugh (1776-1850), builder and wealthy owner of lead mines near Devil's Bridge.

Plate 25. Lewis 'Uncle Pugh' (1810-1868), the bachelor brother of Lewis Evans' mother Eliza Pugh and the donor of the Abermaed estate.

Plate 26. The extravagant house that Lewis and VHP built at Abermaed. The architect was J. P. Seddon and costs overran the original estimate by a factor of three. Inset. Abermaed in 2009.

Plate 27. The wedding of Lewis's brother Griffith Evans (1840-1938) to VHP's sister 'Emmy' Hills (1848-1938), September 4, 1867. VHP's daughter Veronica is second from left among the bridesmaids.

Plate 28. Lewis 'Lal' Pugh Evans (1864-1940), VHP's eldest son.

Plate 29. James Pugh (1870-1895), the wayward second son, who died under strange circumstances.

Plate 30. Archibald Pugh. (b1871), the third son. Colonel of the Calcutta Light Horse Regiment.

Plate 31. VHP with her four daughters. From left; Marjorie (Patterson), Evelyn (Sellar), Veronica (Macnair), 'Nellie' (Ormond).

Plate 32. Herbert Pugh (1874-1950). Fourth son, photographed during the Boer War.

Plate 33. Roland Pugh (1878-1946). The fifth and youngest son.

Plate 34. Veronica Charlotte Evans (1867-1970), who later married 'Jack' Macnair in 1891.

Plate 35. 'Jack' Macnair. (1846-1908) Commanding Officer of the Calcutta Light Horse, scratch golfer and twenty years older than his wife.

Plate 36. VHP's debonair, bachelor brother, 'Charlie' Hills (1847-1935).

Plate 37. Merle Oberon, film star and possibly the daughter of 'Charlie' Hills.

Plate 38. Betha Johnes, younger daughter of the murdered Judge Johnes of Dolaucothi.

Plate 39. Sir 'Jimmy' Hills-Johnes VC with his wife Betha and her elder sister, Mrs Cookson.

Plate 40. Sir Griffith Evans of Lovesgrove in later life.

Plate 41. Lady Evans. Little 'Emmy' Hills is now very much the 'grande dame'.

Plate 42. Col Lewis Evans VC (1881-1962).

Plate 43. General Sir Lewis Evans VC with his kinsman General Lewis Pugh (1907-1981), leader of the daring raid into Goa harbour in 1942, commemorated in the film 'The Sea Wolves'.

Plate 44. Ruth Dent (1898-1984) as a young girl.

Plate 45. James Macnair of Auchinech (1796-1865), father of 'Jack' Macnair.

Plate 46. Ian Macnair (1895-1980) as a 12 year old cadet at Osborne, 1908. He is wearing a black armband in memory of his father who died during a visit to his son.

Plate 47. The marriage of Ian Macnair and Ruth Dent on August 7, 1918, that linked the Hills and Dent families. The reception was held on the lawn of her mother's home, Beacon Corner, Burley, Hampshire. 60 years later they celebrated their diamond wedding anniversary at the same location.

just as the ship sailed, VHP confessed that she had *fallen in love with my new son-in-law*. The newly-weds followed a week later and their first son, James Lewis Pugh Macnair, was baptised at St Paul's Cathedral, Calcutta, on September 16 1892. On February 14 the Calcutta Light Horse held their annual regimental ball at which the newlywed couple danced with the Viceroy and Lady Lansdowne. It would be their last Regimental function, because it had been decided that 'Jack' would run his partnership's London office and that they would now leave India for ever.

But this would not by any means be the end of the family connection with the Calcutta Light Horse Regiment. VHP's third son Col. Archibald Pugh OBE, VD, **[Plate 30]** was the commanding officer from 1912-1922 and during the Second World War her grandson Lewis Owain Pugh, son of Herbert Pugh and at that time a young colonel attached to SOE, the Special Operations Executive, led a group of the Regiment's elderly officers in a daring, clandestine raid against three German ships in the port of Goa in 1942. **[Plate 43]** This crazy venture, code-named 'Operation Longshanks', had to be carried-out in the greatest secrecy because Goa was then owned by the Portuguese and the harbour was neutral territory. The outcome was a spectacular success but the true facts did not emerge until 1978 when James Leasor wrote a book, 'Boarding Party', giving the precise details.[55] Two years later Rank made the swashbuckling film 'The Sea Wolves' which was, apart from two examples of artistic licence, an accurate account of the extraordinary and heroic incident. (The director insisted on including a beautiful young woman as a German spy who killed one of the raiders, when in reality they all returned to their families alive if somewhat battered and bruised.) The film, often repeated on television, starred David Niven, Trevor Howard, Patrick McNee and Roger Moore among other well-known actors, while the role of Lewis Pugh, aged 35 at the time of the exploit, was played by the still very handsome 62 year-old Gregory Peck.

Lewis and VHP were at Abermaed on October 24, 1895, when a bombshell telegram arrived, saying that their second son, James Griffith Pugh, had been killed in Calcutta – but without any details. **[Plate 29]** Lewis and two of the other sons left for India as soon as they could and what they eventually found was a very weird story indeed. The bodies of James Pugh, then aged 25, and a Mr Collingwood, a 32 year-old port-authority pilot, were found in a room at Mr and Mrs Collingwood's house in the small hours of the morning. James Pugh had been shot in the head and Collingwood had been bludgeoned to death by a dumb-bell. A discarded revolver lay nearby. Both men had been close friends and it was initially concluded that they might have been killed in an attempted robbery.[56]

The inquest could not decide whether the two men had been murdered by an intruder or whether, and possibly more likely, the pair had been involved in some drunken game that had gone horribly wrong. But after an adjournment, the jury concluded that James Pugh had killed Mr Collingwood and then 'realising the fatality he had caused, whether intentionally or otherwise, shot himself'. [57] (Rumour had it that James Pugh may have been having an affair with Mrs Collingwood.)

*   *   *   *   *

After this moment of high drama, our story will pause for a moment to catch up with what happened to the two other sons of James Hills who stayed on out in India.

John 'Jack' Hills was, like his brother George, an officer in the Royal Engineers, though he had greater drive and talent and rose to the rank of Major General, being made a Knight Commander of the Bath in 1900. He had been a member of the Persian Expeditionary Force in 1857 and while on sick-leave later that year he was elected as a Fellow of the Royal Society of Edinburgh, the youngest man ever to achieve this distinction. He was then appointed garrison engineer at Fort William, Calcutta, for a time before joining General Napier's force in Abyssinia where he was responsible for building some remarkable mountain roads. He was in command of the Royal Engineer Division at Khandahar, alongside his brother 'Jimmy' Hills, during the Afghan Wars of 1879-81. [58] Of his contribution to this campaign, Sir Henry Cotton recalled that he 'was burly, brusque and good-natured ...... and won fame and honour at the time when all in authority were not so level-headed as himself.'

He had always been short and plump and by now he was, by his own admission, positively fat and quite unable to run. 'There is a tale of his strolling back into Khandahar smoking a large cheroot when General Primrose had ordered a retreat at the double – and the men watched from the walls and cheered the tortoise racing with death.' [59] After his retirement, he wrote two books, the first of which was a lucid account of 'The Bombay Field Force, 1880' in 1900. He had made a lifelong study of horses and in 'The Points of a Racehorse' he drew anatomical comparisons to cheetahs. [60] He died unmarried in 1902.

'Charlie' Hills, the youngest son, was a very different character, renowned in Calcutta for his debonair good looks, his skills at polo and for being the most popular dancing partner. [Plate 36] Sir Henry Cotton wrote of him: 'The last of the brothers was 'Charlie', also in the Calcutta firm of Thomas, as great as 'Bobby' Hills at polo and whom I do not hesitate to describe as the most popular man of his day in Calcutta. I must not omit to add, on the authority of the ladies, that he danced divinely.' He stayed a bachelor all his life though he may have enjoyed a liaison that had a rather startling outcome. His house-keeper in Calcutta was of Anglo-Indian extraction, a 'widow' called Mrs O'Brien, and it has long been rumoured in the family that at the age of 63 he fathered her beautiful daughter – who later changed her name to Merle Oberon and became the renowned film-star. [Plate 37] During her own lifetime she was evasive about the truth of her origins and when she first arrived in Europe, her travelling companion, who she called her *ayah*, was almost certainly her mother.[61] One of the better established facts was that some benefactor had paid for her to have a private education in Calcutta, where she started to make a name for herself in the Amateur Dramatic Society. And it was probably the same sponsor who paid the passage for her and her mother to England in 1929. Veronica Macnair used to tell the story that she went to visit Mrs O'Brien to offer family support but had the door slammed in her face.

'Nellie' Pugh, by now Mrs Ormond, wrote to her brother Herbert Pugh in 1935 confirming that she saw 'a strong family likeness .... I will tell you what Evelyn *(nee Pugh, Mrs Byrne Sellar)* says when I see you. She says there is no doubt of the first-cousinship.' [62] **[Plate 31]** Given the misinformation that surrounded her background and upbringing, the possibility that Merle Oberon was the daughter of 'Charlie' Hills seems as likely as any other. 'Charlie' Hills had always been a fitness fanatic, still doing press-ups well into his eighties and he did not die until 1935.

Chapter 13

A Dynastic Marriage

Veronica and 'Jack' Macnair's second son was born at 27 Phillimore Gardens, London, on May 9, 1895, and christened John Hamilton Macnair though he was always known as Ian. When 'Jack' Macnair retired shortly afterwards, he and Veronica moved to Wales where they rented a house in Pennal, a few miles inland from Aberdovey. This was not far from Veronica's parents and her aunt and uncle, but I suspect that it was the proximity of the golf-links at Aberdovey and the fishing in the River Dovey that swayed her husband's selection. Their daughter Janet arrived in 1902.[63] From an early age both Macnair sons were destined for military careers, James in the army – Royal Artillery – and Ian in the Royal Navy. [64] Ian went to Cordwallis prep-school followed by the naval cadet school at Osborne on the Isle of Wight, the former home of Queen Victoria and Prince Albert.

1908 would prove to be a traumatic year for Veronica, starting with her father's death in Calcutta on January 6. The following day, the *Statesman* newspaper gave Lewis Pugh Evans-Pugh a respectful obituary and the leading article was given over to a review of his life and achievements in two continents, his powers of oratory and his deep knowledge of the law, and expressing regret that neither he nor his brother had accepted the post of Chief Justice. (Sir Griffith Evans had died in 1902, at the relatively early age of 62.) A brass plaque was erected in Calcutta Cathedral to 'The Brothers', recording their loyal public service as members of the Legislative Council of the Government of India. But for Veronica, worse was to come. On March 12, she and her husband were visiting their son Ian at Osborne when 'Jack' Macnair suffered a massive heart attack and died. This coincided with Ian being on stand-by to be called as a witness in the famous 'Archer-Shee' court of enquiry (later made into a play, 'The Winslow Boy', by Terence Rattigan) so he was never actually summoned to give evidence, though he had been in the post-office at the time of the crucial signing of a postal order that lay at the heart of the case. At the age of 41, Veronica suddenly found herself a widow with the responsibility of bringing up three children on very limited resources.

Ian Macnair **[Plate 46]** progressed from Osborne to HMS *Britannia* at Dartmouth and on the outbreak of the First World War he was posted as a midshipman on board HMS *Inflexible*, one of the navy's mighty new battle-cruisers. He saw his first action at the Battle of the Falkland Islands in December 1914, when a British squadron under Admiral Sturdee won a convincing and decisive battle over the German force commanded by Admiral Von Spee. Only one German cruiser managed to escape from the annihilation while the British ships suffered little damage and few casualties. Ian wrote a long and excited letter to his mother describing what he had been able to see of the action and the subsequent operation to rescue German survivors from the water. His training had instilled in him the 'Nelson spirit' and an unquestioning sense of duty to God, King and Empire, mollified by a chivalrous respect for the enemy's sailors. 'The German officers that we picked up,' he wrote, 'were awfully nice fellows and it was very interesting hearing all about the action from their side.' [65]

June 1915 found Ian, still on HMS *Inflexible*, involved in the less successful fleet action at Jutland and an appalled witness to the dramatic sinking of their sister-ship HMS *Invincible*, as he recorded in another letter home. 'She was leading the line at the time and we were just astern of her. Then at half-past six a whole salvo hit her and must have got into one of the magazines because she just blew up. It was a tremendous sight!' [66] Then it was off to the Dardanelles and shelling the Turkish forts in support of the reckless landings at Gallipoli.

He was on leave at Rosyth on the Firth of Forth in 1917 when he received an invitation to tea in Edinburgh from an elderly lady whom he had never met but knew of as a rather distant relation. Eleanor Sellar was the widow of Walter Sellar, the Professor of Humanities at Edinburgh University, whose brother Thomas Sellar had married an American called Adele Byrne. One of their sons, Thomas Byrne Sellar became an officer in the King's Own Scottish Borderers and had married Ian's aunt, his mother's sister Evelyn Pugh.

Ian had invested his meagre pay on a primitive motorcycle that he had christened 'Boanerges' (one of the 'sons of thunder') and it was on this noisy machine that he turned up at 15 Buckingham Terrace. In her memoirs, Dr. Poldores McCunn, a granddaughter of Eleanor Sellar, recalled the house and its occupants around that time. [67]

It is difficult to imagine why my grandmother spent some sixty years of her life in 15 Buckingham Terrace. The house faces north and even in midsummer the sun never shone into the drawing-room and dining-room; it is inconveniently situated on the far side of the windswept Dean Bridge and it contains four floors and a basement. By the time I can remember it, the household consisted of Grannie herself, Aunt Carlo [*her eldest, spinster daughter, 'a great traveller and socialite who exuded disapproval'*] and Uncle Edmund, a tea planter who had been invalided home from Ceylon; the staff had boiled down to cook, kitchen-maid, housemaid, Grannie's personal maid Quinton and Fanny, the redoubtable table-maid.

Not mentioned was another house-guest, Eleanor Sellar's other granddaughter Ruth Dent, who was an art student. Ruth was just 18, the only child of May Sellar who had married a Capt. Edgar Dent, also of the KOSBs. **[Plate 48]** He had been invalided home from the Boer War and had dropped down dead in the Caledonian Railway Hotel in 1906 when Ruth was only six. She was a rather shy girl and had led a sheltered upbringing with her widowed mother and nanny. **[Plate 44]** Her education had come from a governess, who had stimulated her interest in literature and encouraged her early talent for drawing and painting, which is why it had been decided that she should go and stay with her grandmother and enrol in the Edinburgh Art School. She happened to be coming down the stairs at 15 Buckingham Terrace when Ian Macnair was ushered into the hall, their eyes met and, to use a hackneyed phrase, 'it was love at first sight'. In truth though, it was the start of a love-affair that lasted for sixty-two years.

More meetings were arranged during Ian's leave and the couple very quickly decided that they wanted to become engaged. But marriage was out of the question, because neither had any money and the Navy did not sanction marriage allowances until officers were over the age of 25. So Ian's first move was to volunteer for service in submarines, then a particularly hazardous occupation that paid an extra 3 shillings and 4 pence a day 'danger money'. He was assigned to one of Admiral Fisher's very large, experimental K class submarines that were powered, on the surface, by steam. With a speed of 30 knots, they were like submersible destroyers and they were designed to be able to keep up with the Fleet battleships and take part in set-piece battles like that at Jutland. It took them seven minutes to prepare for diving while all the holes in the hull, such as the funnels and the ventilators, were sealed watertight. The residual heat from the boilers made them hellish places under water. [68]

Several of the 'K-boats' were sunk in a notorious training exercise off the Island of May in the Firth of Forth on the night of January 31, 1918, when fog came down, communication was lost and four of the submarines were rammed by speeding cruisers, including HMS *Inflexible*. [69] Two boats were sunk and 103 sailors drowned. Ian's vessel was one of the unfortunate ones but, by a stroke of luck, he was not on board at the time but confined to the naval hospital with mumps.

By the summer of 1918 Ian and Ruth decided that they could not bear to wait any longer and they were married from her mother's home in the New Forest on

August 7. **[Plate 47]** Sixty years later they would celebrate their diamond wedding anniversary on the same lawn and the guests used the very same glasses to drink their health. Each recognised in the other the mutual bond of having lost their fathers at a young age and throughout their marriage they could not bear to be parted. Ian continued his career in the Royal Navy, in submarines till 1930 and then in command of a succession of destroyers. In 1936, he was the senior officer of the Gibraltar Defence Flotilla, in command of HMS *Shamrock,* and his dashing exploits during the opening weeks of the Spanish Civil War are recorded in a book published in 2007. [70] This book reveals for the first time his 'secret' missions to rescue refugees from Malaga and Seville and his contentious meeting with Franco's General Queippo de Llano, exploits never recorded in the official history of the Royal Navy. He was at sea throughout the Second World War, captaining a minelayer and then serving as Flag Captain to the admiral in charge of the naval bombardment during the D-Day landings, for which he was mentioned in despatches. His final command was to take HMS *Tyne* out to Burma in 1945 where he became C-in-C Akiab.

During the inter-war years, Ruth 'followed the fleet' whenever she could, often leaving their two daughters to be looked after by her mother. (Some of her adventures are recalled in a later chapter in Book 2.) On their 16th wedding anniversary, when Ian was at sea, he wrote a sonnet for Ruth which ended as follows; [71]

You stole my heart on an Edinburgh stair
and there's a tale begun!
But oh my love, it seems hardly fair,
whenever a day we cannot share,
to steal the sparkle out of the air
and the splendour out of the sun.

May Sellar, Mrs Dent, the old lady I knew as 'Granny Dent', frequently reminisced about her own childhood in Victorian Edinburgh and her time as one of the first girl undergraduates at St. Leonards College, later absorbed into St Andrews University. How she had studied German and translated folk tales from that country for her cousin, the poet Andrew Lang for publication in his popular anthologies of fairy-stories. But she never spoke of her married life, nor of her late husband Capt. Edgar Dent who remained a misty figure in my upbringing, a faded photograph at the back of her writing desk. **[Plate 48]** As far as I understood it, he had had a fairly normal military career, fighting under General Kitchener during the Sudan Wars and then in the Boer War. His own father had also been an army officer, in the elite Madras Cavalry, before retiring to England and marrying into the Huddlestone family, landed gentry from Ormskirk in Lancashire. All very proper and utterly respectable, so why the veil of silence and the aura of mystery?

Granny Dent's income arose from a trust administered by the small but exclusive bank of Child & Co. with its single branch at 1 Fleet St., London. Childs had once been the Royal bank back in the 17th century and the connection came somehow through the Dent family. What nobody mentioned, and what I only discovered fairly recently, was that the source of the Dent money was tainted, stained by its uncomfortable origin in commodity trading from India into China during the 19th century. And that commodity was opium.

Endnotes and References

1   Anderson. They were united by one genetic trait, both being left-handed – hence the Scottish term 'kerhanded'. The main staircase in Ferniehurst Castle was built for left-handed defenders.

2   Fraser.

3   Parish Records. For some reason unknown, possible a deaf rector, her name is spelt as Kar.

4   According to the Parish Records of Eckford, Walter Ker had been born 'in the map tower' in February 1723. He married Bessie Scott of Wilton on November 29, 1747. In the unpublished memoirs of J-J Evans written in the 1920s, he states that General Walter Ker did have a son, who pre-deceased him, though whether he was by Walter Ker's wife Bessie or his second wife Jane Forster (married supposedly in 1797) is not made clear.

5   My grandmother, Veronica Macnair (nee Evans), claimed that she discovered the 'marriage lines' while researching some family archives in the 1940s and had sent them to the then Duke of Buccleugh – without taking a copy first. She never had a reply.

6   VHP. This and all subsequent extracts from the Memoirs of Veronica Harriet Hills will be shown in italics.

7   PM.

8   From Halterburn, they migrated to 12 Gilmour Place in Edinburgh where Archibald became a land-agent, managing, among others, some estates for the Jardine family in Dumfriesshire. An interesting coincidence providing another link between the two halves of this book.

9   VHP.

10 Gaetano Savi (1769-1844) taught physics and botany at the University of Pisa while his son Paolo (1798-1871) became the Professor of Botany and is acknowledged as the 'father of Italian geology'.

11 From the minutes of the court-martial of Captain Roddam Home RN.

12 Like Pondicherry, it changed hands frequently during the local Anglo-French campaigns after 1740, being taken for a third time by the British in 1794 when the Napoleonic conflict in Europe went global. It was restored to the French after the Treaty of Vienna in 1816 by which time Dr Angelo Savi was recorded as a 'foreign resident' on the ledgers of the EIC.

13 LPP.

14 Ibid. A title-deed for a house in the Calcutta records is also signed by him as 'Sage, dit Savi.'

15 These were later developed as a club and resort for British army officers in the 1880s.

16 By the middle of the 19th century, some steam powered machinery was introduced to mechanise the aeration and filtration areas, reducing the most dangerous and labour intensive parts of the process.

17 This might well be a portrait of Captain Charles Elliott – see Book 2 – though in fact it shows Admiral Sir George Cockburn (1772-1853), commander of the fleet that sacked Washington in 1814 during the Anglo-American War.

18 Greer, A.

19 AH.

20 Arthur William Devis (1762-1822). When sold in 1972, it fetched £26,000 and was believed in some quarters, erroneously, to have been painted by Zoffany. (*The Times*, March 23, 1972.)

21 *Indian Journal of History of Science,* 19 (3), 1984, pp215-223.

22 Balfour-Paul, p72. The main consuming countries were (chests); England 11,500, France 8,000, Germany and the rest of Europe 13,500, Persia 3,500, United States 2,000, all other countries, including China, 4,500.

23 Kling, p21.

24 Cotton.

25 Dubus.

26 VHP. Charlotte was converted to the Protestant faith during this visit.

27 *Budgerow.* 'A large and commodious, but generally cumbrous and sluggish boat, used for journeys on the Ganges'.

28 The Suez canal was only opened in 1869.

29 Kling pp27 & 59.

30 The VC medal won by 'Jimmy' Hills, later General Sir James Hills-Johnes, is now in the FIREPOWER Museum at Woolwich. (See rear cover.)

31 Chinhut was 8 miles to the east of Lucknow, the headquarters of General Sir Henry Lawrence. Lawrence had taken a force of 800 to try and relieve the garrison at Cawnpore but ran into a force of about 15,000 rebels at Chinhut and was forced to withdraw with heavy losses.

32 Kling.

33 Kling, p193.

34 About £200, or £12,000 at today's values.

35 The broad-gauge railway had been built to improve land communications with Burma (via Dacca), so that Indian troops would not have to travel 'overseas' and

thereby lose their caste. The consulting engineer was Isambard Kingdom Brunel – one of his last projects.

36 Gastrell & Blauford. They also report that at least 25,000 people died subsequently from cholera and dysentery.

37 LPP.

38 Elizabeth Garrett finally obtained a full medical degree from the Sorbonne University of Paris in 1870, becoming the first female doctor in the UK. The following year she married the shipping magnate James Anderson, who became her staunchest supporter in her campaign for the advancement of women in the medical profession and later helped her found the London School of Medicine for Women. Her sister Agnes Garrett (Fawcett) became a famous furniture designer and another sister, Millicent, achieved fame as the leader of the National Union of Women's Suffrage.

39 Greer.

40 Research by Veronica Macnair and Phyllida Mould (nee Ormond) based partly on the 'Heraldic Visitations of Wales' by Lewys Dwnn in the reign of Queen Elizabeth, edited by Sir Samuel Rush, and published by the Society for the Publication of Ancient Welsh manuscripts, 1846. It included a somewhat mythical ancestry of the ancient Pughs that stretched back through Aeneas of Troy to Adam himself.

41 Pevsner, in *The Buildings of Wales*, (edited by Tom Lloyd) described it as follows. 'The best High Victorian house in the region and one of the most interesting of its period, for this is a compact demonstration of modern Gothic, the functional ideas of Pugin contrast to Seddons' fantastical Castle Hotel of the same period.' The latter went bankrupt within a year of its opening.

42 His Will had been witnessed on 13 March, 1871, empowering his trustees to sell his indigo factories or continue to run them as going concerns. After all his debts had been settled, he bequeathed 20,000 rupees to Emmy, his only unmarried daughter, 5,000 rupees each to his son Charlie and his sister Tomima, and 3,000 rupees to 'Tottie' Cubitt. Any balance to be equalled divided among all his children. In the event, after paying off the mortgages and legal fees in India, it is doubtful if there was much for the residual legatees. (*Research by A Chalmers Hills 1982, who estimated that the rupee was worth about £1 in 1871.*)

43 Ernest Ormond married VHP's daughter 'Nellie' in 1896 and they had three children; Charles, Herbert and 'Jack'.

44 Grave number 23600, in plot 153/RS. Epitaphs on the gravestone for other members of the family are; his children: 1) Archibald Hills d.1896, buried in Calcutta. 2) Major General Sir John Hills d. 1902. 3) Colonel George Scott Hills d. 1892. 4) Charles Hills d.1934. 5) Elizabeth Scott Hills d.1897 and 6) her

husband Lt. General Jenkin Jones RE d 1903. Their sons: 6) Major Jenkin Jones d.1918. 7) Harry Jones d. 1925 and 8) James Hills Jones d. 1902.

45 Cotton, pp80-87.

46 Marjorie married Alexander Patterson and they had four children.

47 Oxford History of India.

48 Lewis 'Lal' Pugh went on to be a successful barrister at the Calcutta Bar. He married Adah Chaplin in 1896 and they had five daughters and one son, Griffith Pugh, born in 1909. He grew up to become an Olympic skier, doctor and physiologist, specialising in high altitude medicine. He was a crucial member of the team that first conquered Everest in 1953. (Harriet Tuckey, 'Everest – the first ascent' published by Rider, 2013.)

49 LPP. The mine continued to operate until the 1920s under a succession of owners. Records show that the number of miners employed varied between 65 in 1907 and 200 in 1912. (Pwll Perkins website.)

50 CE. Money matters put a severe strain on the two brothers/sisters relationship. 'Emmy' wrote to her son in 1901; 'Dad seems depressed by money affairs as Abermaed will have to be sold. Uncle Lewis is doing so badly with his money that there seems little chance of us being paid back anything of what Dad has lent him.'

51 This was the second oldest golf club in the world outside Scotland. Founded in 1827, the course was originally situated at Dum-Dum, north of Calcutta, but moved to its present location near the Tollygunge Club in the 1920s, when the land was compulsorily purchased to make way for the airport. The two gold medals won by 'Jack' Macnair were inherited by the author, who presented them to his own golf-club, Blackwell, Worcs., They are competed for in an annual foursomes match, the 'Macnair Calcutta Trophy', after an alcohol-fuelled curry lunch.

52 In the author's possession.

53 *Calcutta Light Horse*, published by Gale & Polden, 1957. Compiled by a committee of members of the regiment after its disbandment in 1947. This includes an interesting photograph taken in 1893 at the annual camp which suggests that the inspecting officer had been Lord 'Bobs' Roberts VC.

54 MM family records.

55 Leasor.

56 *The Englishman* and *The Indian Daily News*, Calcutta, October 25, 1895.

57 *The Englishman,* Calcutta, October 28, 1895.

58 Col. R. Vetch, the *Royal Engineers Journal*, November 1911.

59 Greer.

60 The book was published by Blackwood in 1903, the year he died.

61 In the biography of Merle Oberon *('Merle', by Charles Higham and Roy Moseley, New English Library, 1983)* it is stated that Merle was born in Bombay on February 19, 1911. Her 28 year old mother, Charlotte Selby, 'part Irish, part Singhalese with Maori strains in her blood' had become pregnant in Poona, and had persuaded one of her many lovers to marry her, an engineer by the name of Arthur Terence O'Brien Thompson. She later told Merle that her father had been 'a ship's captain who never came home', later changing the story to 'an army major, who had died of pneumonia on a hunting trip'. Also Barker, C. ODNB.

62 Letter in the possession of Phylidda Mould (nee Ormond.).

63 Janet never married, devoting her life to looking after her mother and organising the Montgomeryshire Field Society, later being elected as its president.

64 James Macnair.

65 Now in the archives of the Imperial War Museum.

66 Ibid.

67 Unpublished; in the author's possession. Poldores was the daughter of Florence McCunn (nee Sellar), Professor Sellar's third child.

68 Everitt.

69 An account of the 'Battle of May Island' was published in *The Scotsman*, Jan 30, 1988. See also Everitt.

70 *Witness to War*, edited by Miles Macnair, Brewin Books 2007. This book reveals for the first time his missions to rescue refugees from Malaga and Seville, and his meeting with Franco's General Queippo de Llano, exploits never recorded in the official history of the Royal Navy.

71 *Poems* by Ian Macnair, an anthology of 45 poems written between 1914 and 1978, edited by his daughter Eleanor Macnair and printed privately. Several had been published in 'Country Life' magazine.

Book Two

THE DENT SAGA

Chapter 1

China and Tea

Edgar Dent's great-uncle was Lancelot Dent, a tough, buccaneering entrepreneur. **[Plate 57]** [1] During the early 1830s, he saw himself as a pioneering trader opening up markets for the British Empire into China via Canton (Guangzhou), while the East India Company looked upon him as an unofficial and unorthodox agent of their business, one who played a crucial role in balancing their books. He made himself a considerable fortune. And in 1839 he was very largely responsible for striking the spark that ignited the tinder-box of war, dragging the British Government into military conflict with China, a war whose spoils would add Hong Kong as another diadem in the imperial crown of Queen Victoria.

How and why had Lancelot Dent gone to Canton? And how had he managed to become so rich? To unravel the answers to these questions we first of all need to delve into the history of China's opaque relationship with the outside world at that time.

China – Cathay – the mysterious Orient, land of dragons and demons, of mighty rivers and an even mightier Emperor who lived in a Forbidden City, guarded by a thousand eunuchs. Early travellers and explorers told tales of gilded temples with statues of monstrous creatures called the 'Dogs of Fo'; how the people had yellow skins and slanted eyes and wore their hair in pigtails; how high-born women had their feet tightly bound from birth so that they could not run away from their husbands, and how their black-hulled ships used slatted sails that resembled the wings of great sea-eagles. Tales of untold riches and a mighty wall that stretched for over 4,000 miles, taller than most buildings in London. To people living in England at the end of the 18th century, it was the great, isolated, impenetrable enigma, from which emerged along the Silk Routes of Central Asia, on the backs of camels, luxurious goods of great beauty and value; silks, spices, rhubarb and paintings of strange flowers, exotic birds and misty mountain ranges, polished lacquer-work in black and red and the eponymous ceramic with its translucent lustre that the French called porcelain. 'Chinoiserie' became the height of fashion. China was also the only source of the magic tea plant, whose leaves could be brewed in boiling water to produce a delightful stimulating potion.

It was known that in years gone by the Chinese had invented the printing press, the machine that had revolutionised the dissemination of knowledge, and gunpowder, the product that changed the nature of warfare forever. This rich, inventive nation must surely be ripe to open its doors to the new technical marvels that were emerging from the factories of Britain's burgeoning Industrial Revolution. But it was not going to be as easy as it might seem to ambitious traders like Lancelot Dent. It was not so much a problem with the quality of the goods they could offer but one of diplomatic protocol and ignorance of the complete contempt in which the Chinese Imperial Court held all foreigners. 'The Chinese system of Government was Confucian in origin and peculiar in character. The Emperor ruled "all below heaven" ...... and ambassadors and envoys from abroad were treated as tribute bearers.' [2]

So it was somewhat ironic that the ruling dynasty in the capital Peking (Beijing) were foreign invaders themselves from China's northern borders. The warlike tribe of the Manchus had invaded in 1644 and overthrown the Ming dynasty of the indigenous Han people, usurping the Celestial Throne and starting their own dynasty, 'the Qing'. It would never enjoy universal popular support and over the following centuries, until its final collapse in 1912, would have to face a succession of internal uprisings and fight off invaders that threatened its western land frontiers. Anyone approaching from the sea was perceived as a potential enemy.

The first foothold for maritime trade by Europeans into China was established in Macau, a small peninsular on the west side of the entrance to the Pearl River in south China. It was leased from the Chinese as a trading post by the Portuguese in the 16th century, with sovereignty still retained by China until it became a colony of the European state in 1887. The local Portuguese administration jealously guarded their monopoly of the sea-borne trade between India and their overlords, who sent trading vessels down the river from the walled city of Canton that lay seventy miles upstream. In 1622, the Dutch tried to invade and capture the settlement as part of their plans to extend their sphere of influence from the East Indies. Beaten off by a make-shift local militia consisting largely of African slaves who stayed loyal to their Portuguese masters, the Dutch withdrew and would never again be allowed to establish a foothold on the Chinese coast. Meanwhile, the East India Company (EIC) had been granted a monopoly of all British trade to the Far East under the terms of its original charter of 1600, but when it sent its first merchant ship to Macau in 1673 it was refused entry.

In 1699, however, the EIC's *Macclesfield* was allowed to trade its cargo of woollen goods for tea, silk and porcelain and over the following two decades one EIC ship a year was allowed to repeat the process. Transhipment of goods at Macau was inefficient for both the Chinese and the EIC, quite apart from the fact that Macau harbour was shallow and the anchorage unprotected from the violent storms that were common in the region. So in 1720 the Chinese merchants formed a guild to be known as the 'Co-Hong' and the sole point of trade was shifted, for purely administrative reasons, up the river to the outskirts of Canton, then the largest city in the world. Here, on the north bank of the river opposite the island of Hanan, under the walls of the city, the Chinese allowed selected foreigners, including the EIC, to build their first warehouses, *godowns*. But trade was almost completely one-sided. The Chinese expressed very little interest in what the EIC could offer while the British were increasingly desperate to get their hands on a commodity that was then unique to China – namely tea.

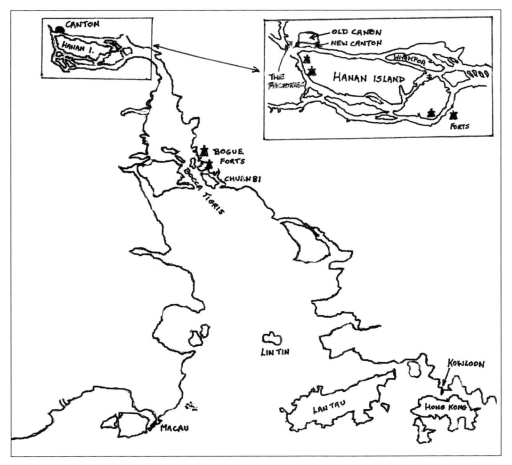

Map 3. Sketch map of the Pearl River estuary, showing the location of Canton in relation to Macau and Hong Kong. Also Lin Tin island and the Bogue forts guarding the Bocca Tigris narrows.

Tea had been introduced into England via King Charles II's wife, the Portuguese Princess Catherine of Braganza, quickly becoming the fashionable drink of the aristocracy by the end of the 17th century. Soon however its appeal filtered down the social order until it became an indispensable brew for the middle classes and artisans as well. Water supply in the expanding cities was increasingly suspect and a drink that demanded the water to be boiled, and therefore sterilised, was a recipe for health as well as pleasure. Certainly compared to gin, and to a lesser extent beer and ale, it was ethically acceptable as well. By 1750, consumption of tea in England amounted to 12 million pounds weight per annum, for which the Chinese demanded £6 million – in silver. And not even silver bullion; settlement had to be made before shipment and in the form of uncirculated Mexican/Spanish Dollar coins. When demand exceeded availability, these acquired a premium price. This trade imbalance was accentuated by the time that cargoes took to reach England from the Far East; several months depending on winds and weather. Many an argosy never reached its destination, either being wrecked in storms or captured by pirates that infested the seas off the China coast and through the Straits of Malaca.

The shift in trade to Canton had a very deleterious effect on the economy of Macau, so in 1757 the Portuguese administration relaxed its rules on foreigners setting up residence there, no longer demanding that anyone wishing to do so must adopt Portuguese nationality. Three years later, the rules applying to trade between the 'Co-Hong' and foreign traders into China were formalised into a set of understandings that became known as the 'Eight Regulations'. Canton was to be the only trading port. Foreigners were not allowed within the walls of Canton itself but had to live within the compounds of their warehouses – referred to as 'factories', not because anything was made within them but because the traders, including a high-proportion of Scotsmen, were agents or, to use the Scottish term, 'factors'. This foreign enclave on the riverbank to the south-west of the old walls became known as 'Faqi-city'.

No wives or families were allowed, nor any armaments, and no warship could enter the Pearl River past the defensive Bogue forts at the Bocca Tigris ('mouth of the tiger'), about 30 miles downstream. There was a strict six-month trading season, by which time all business had to be completed and debts settled and after which the traders had to depart, for India or Macau. All trade had to be channelled through the 'Co-Hong' together with any petitions to Government officials. These rules were strictly enforced, but the one which was supposed to prevent the traders employing Chinese servants or translators was very largely overlooked and allowed to wither by default. When Lancelot and Wilkinson Dent arrived in the 1820s to join their elder brother Thomas Dent, the 'Eight Regulations' still applied.

The first formal diplomatic mission from Britain to the Imperial Court in Peking was sent from the EIC in London in 1793. Headed by Lord Macartney and a retinue of noblemen, it had the blessing of King George III, whose portrait was taken proudly into the audience finally granted to the delegation, after much hanging around in waiting rooms. It got off to a very bad start from which it never recovered and achieved absolutely nothing except to convince those on both sides that their opposite numbers were stubborn, uncivilised and living in a different world. The immediate stumbling-block was that the British were expected, like every other visitor to the presence of the Emperor, the self-confessed Son of Heaven, to 'kow-tow', fall prostrate to the ground and kiss the floor at the foot of the Celestial Throne. A step too far for the dignity of Lord Macartney and his delegation, who turned on their heels and departed.

It was supposed to have been largely a trade mission, with expectations of persuading the powers that be to open trade routes for the import of English manufactured goods – cotton cloth from India and woollen goods, clocks and watches, ingenious toys and other machinery from England. The Emperor, the haughty, philosopher grandee Qianlong, sent a personal letter back with the angry and crest-fallen Lord Macartney in which he declared; 'Our ways have no resemblance to yours – strange and costly objects do not interest me'. The mandarins and their civil servants wore furs and silk, ate out of porcelain bowls with ivory chop-sticks and surrounded themselves with golden ornaments and silk paintings, while entertaining themselves by writing poetry. Why should they want scratchy wool, inferior pottery, musical boxes and Sheffield cutlery that required the use of two hands to eat? The rest of the population were peasants who eked out an existence in serfdom, an existence devoted entirely to the daily struggle of striving to grow enough food to stay alive. There was no social class in between. Working in the Civil Service was the ambition of all intelligent Chinese and for this the stringent entrance exams concentrated on philosophy, calligraphy and poetry composition rather than economics or administration. To Confucian ideology, trade was a lowly, demeaning and unworthy occupation.

Another delegation, under the guise of diplomacy but with improvement in terms for trade as its underlying mission, was sent out to Peking in 1816 under Lord Amherst. Once again the refusal to 'kow-tow' proved to be an insurmountable obstacle and his party were not even allowed within the city gates. The portrait of King George III that he was supposed to give the Emperor ended up on the far wall of the EIC dining room in the foreign enclave at Canton, opposite that of Lord Amherst himself once he had been appointed Governor General of India in succession to Warren Hastings in 1823.

If the Chinese claimed that they had no need of what Britain could offer them, the British had developed this demand for enormous quantities of tea, leading to a serious deficit in the balance of trade between the two countries. Between 1800 and 1810, the net inflow of cash into China amounted to $26 million; this was crippling the finances of the EIC and hence impinging on the Treasury back in London. There was just one commodity that China did have a demand for, and in very large quantities, a product that was surrounded by a host of issues that were quite distinct from the economics of production, transport and supply, issues that involved both social demand and moral acceptability. This commodity was opium. And to understand how this came about we need to backtrack into the history of this extraordinary substance, praised in some quarters as a miracle, life saving medicine and demonised in others as a pernicious narcotic that could steal men's souls.

Chapter 2

Opium

The therapeutic merits of poppy seeds were known to the ancient Egyptians; the ancient Greeks knew and wrote about their narcotic properties. When Socrates was condemned to death in 399BC, the executioner loaded the fatal dose of hemlock with a mass of ground poppy seeds so that his mind would be numbed before the poison struck his internal organs. It was in the Middle East, sometime in the Middle Ages, that people discovered how the essence of the poppy's secret was contained in the milky latex that exuded from cuts made into the flesh of the ripening seed-heads. Particularly those of one particular poppy, *papaver somniferum*. The latex could be scraped off by hand, collected and then dried, to give a dark brown ball of slightly resinous powder. When crushed and diluted with various liquids, a drinkable potion was produced. Across subsequent ages and around the whole world, both serious doctors and charlatan 'quacks' contrived their own formulations for which they would claim miracle cures for ailments ranging from cholera to headaches, from stomach pains to impotence. A Chinese medical manual of the 8th century extolled the virtues of opium for treating diarrhoea and dysentery as well as arthritis, malaria and what is now known as athlete's foot. During the Ming dynasty (1368-1644) opium-enhanced aphrodisiacs became the height of fashion and probably contributed to the early deaths of eleven of the Ming Emperors, though whether this high mortality was due to overindulgence or assassination is open to question. [3]

Opium mixed with alcohol was known in Europe as laudanum. From the Victorian era onwards, dilute concoctions were happily purchased by mothers to help send querulous children to peaceful sleep, while no middle-class medicine cupboard would be without a bottle of Dr Collis Browne's foul-tasting Chlorodyne. In the right hands, opium based medicines certainly worked, often with unique effectiveness. The 'sleepy sponge', thrust into the mouth of anyone undergoing surgery, made life more tolerable for both patient and surgeon. Thomas Sydenham, often referred to as the 'father of English medicine', is quoted as saying: 'Among the remedies which it has pleased Almighty God to give to man to relieve his sufferings, none is so universal and effective as opium.' The eminent Austrian doctor Ignac Semmelweis told his students that 'without opium, I would not want to be a doctor', a sentiment that was probably echoed by most practitioners.

It was opium's ability to diminish pain that was its most rewarding medical value. (Later in the 19th century the underlying opiate chemicals would be extracted and refined to make morphine – and heroin.) Patients felt better even if the underlying disease was not cured and this self-induced therapy was itself a powerful assistant to restoring health. It was equally appreciated and understood that overdosing could be fatal as the soothing medicine turned into a virulent poison. Dosage at intermediate levels induced a joyful state of day-dreaming euphoria and was adopted by many artists, authors and poets to stimulate their imaginations, famous examples being Samuel Coleridge's 'Xanadu' and Thomas de Quincy's 'Confessions of an opium eater'. Alfred Lord Tennyson probably never indulged, but his 1832 poem 'The Lotus-eaters' reflects the generally tolerant attitude to those that did. Spirits would be raised and depression could be lifted, though many doctors recorded that the after effect, the let-down, affected different patients in different ways; in the case of patients with a natural tendency to morbidity the subsequent state could be worse than the first. To many moralists opium was far preferable to alcohol, as expounded by Rev. Walter Colton in 1836. [4]

> If a man will take stimulants, the juice of the poppy has strong recommendations. It never makes a man foolish; it never casts a man into a ditch or under a table; it never deprives him of his wits or his legs. It allows a man to be a Gentleman; it makes him a visionary, and his visions create no noise or riots, they deal no blows, blacken no one's eye and threaten no one's peace.

It was in Chinese court circles that an alternative method of absorbing opium was devised, namely by smoking it in a pipe. Tobacco had been introduced to the country by Dutch traders in the early 18th century and it was not long before certain mandarins found that the stimulating, narcotic effect of inhaling tobacco smoke could be enhanced by mixing it with locally grown opium. And the tobacco element was soon discarded as being unnecessary. The practice acquired its own ritual, like the Japanese tea ceremony, with elaborate paraphernalia, beautiful storage jars and ever more costly pipes; it became an essential element in the post-prandial routine of court officials. One Emperor had a chef dedicated solely to preparing his pipe mixture. It was not long before the pleasures of the opium pipe filtered down to all levels of the Chinese Civil Service and the myriads of servants employed by the mandarins. While the mandarins used it for recreational delight to unlock their poetic muses, soldiers and peasants resorted to the habit as a release from their unending tedium and the brutality of their daily existence. But the strain of poppy indigenous to China produced a weak, feeble extract compared to that offered by the earliest European traders, and their Chinese counterparts quickly realised that here, potentially, lay the basis for hugely profitable business.

In Europe the main source of opium was Turkey, where a particularly powerful strain of the poppy grew wild in Anatolia. But it was soon found that *papaver somniferum* flourished exceptionally well when grown in India, along the valley of the Ganges in Bengal and Bihar. The EIC stimulated cultivation to supply this new and rewarding market. [5] Soon the habit had spread to a large proportion of the Chinese army, whose soldiers became increasingly reluctant to fight in the endless border disputes, while mandarins had to come to terms with the fact that their servants were perpetually sozzled. The Emperor Yong Zheng had tried, with little

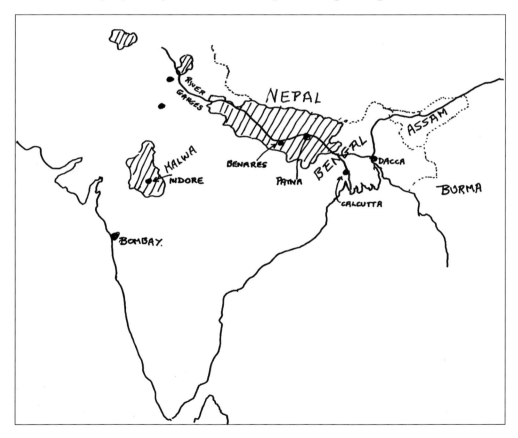

Map 4. Sketch map of the Ganges valley and the principal opium growing areas in northern India. The shaded portions shows cultivation areas of more than 1,000 acres where poppies represented between 1 and 5 percent of all crops.

effect, to prohibit the sale of opium except for medicinal purposes in 1729; his successor, Emperor Jiaqing, became so worried by the state of affairs in 1799 that an order forbidding the import of opium was issued, and reinforced by an Imperial edict. 'That our countrymen should pursue this destructive and ensnaring vice is odious and deplorable,' adding that 'foreigners obviously derive the most solid profits and advantages (from it).'

What the edict neglected to say or admit was that the largest profits of all were being made by the Chinese officials and merchants handling the importation, who accepted bribes from the captains of the ships that brought the opium chests into Canton and 'squeeze' money from the traders who distributed them on. It is ironic to realise that if Lord Macartney had been able to open a dialogue with the Emperor in 1793, one of the concessions he had been prepared to offer in exchange for wider trade opportunities was strict regulation of opium exports from Calcutta. And he had both the mandate and the means to do this because earlier that year the EIC had enforced their monopoly on all opium growing in Bengal and the other regions, like Bihar and Orissa, which came under the company's authority after the defeat of the French at Plassey in 1775. The EIC not only controlled the cultivation but also established large drying sheds, the final process being to mould the raw opium into balls weighing approximately 3lbs each, wrap them in poppy leaves and pack them in batches of 40-45 into wooden chests. (Each chest ended up weighing 1 picul, a rather vague unit of weight based on the maximum amount that two men could carry on a shoulder pole.) Opium produced from the hinterland of Bombay, known as 'Malwar', was of even greater potency and so commanded a higher price and each ball was packed into a shell of baked clay.

The edict of 1799 put the EIC in a dilemma. They simply could not give up the income from opium production since it provided the main source of revenue to counter the imbalance of the tea trade. On the other hand, they still held out hopes of expanding the range of goods offered for Chinese consumption and needed to appease the Emperor accordingly. The answer the EIC came up with was Machiavellian and, like the Roman God Janus, faced in two directions at once. They declared, making sure it was known at the Imperial Palace, that the company, 'Honest John', would never again undertake the *export* of opium. At the same time they made it known in Calcutta and Bombay that they maintained the monopoly for growing and processing opium and that anyone wishing to purchase the stuff had to buy it off the company – with payment up front. **[Plate 62]** Such purchasers would have to act completely independently of any connection with the company and became known as 'country agents'. The EIC's monopoly was partially revoked by the British Government under the Charter Act of 1813, though trade with China and that in tea were unaffected. Opium imports into Canton during the 1818 trading season amounted to 4,000 chests. By 1833-4, this figure had risen to 30,000 and in time opium would be the single largest traded commodity anywhere in the world (see Appendix A).

So this is how and why bold, risk taking, fortune-seeking entrepreneurs like Lancelot Dent, and his great rivals William Jardine and James Matheson, would appear on the scene. What they would undertake was officially disowned at one end of the supply chain and branded as illegal at the other. They had, by force of circumstance, to become smugglers. They sold their opium to the Chinese in exchange for silver and then, back in Calcutta, swapped the bullion for Bills of Exchange redeemable in London. And they had to beat off competition from other rival agents, including Parsees from India and American ships bringing Turkish opium from Smyrna. Traders out of India, however, did have one vital advantage in their favour because the EIC monopoly rules meant that every chest of opium exported from Calcutta or Bombay was stamped with the EIC 'seal of quality' symbol, one that the Chinese importers held in very high regard indeed. To them the seal of the 'Honest John' company guaranteed that the product would not be adulterated by sand or sawdust or other contaminants and could therefore command a premium price.

Lancelot Dent achieved his success to a large extent by his single-minded determination, but he also started off with the advantage of family patronage and a network of relations already associated with banking in London and trade in the Far-East. These were not aristocratic connections and indeed the background to the Dent family was distinctly modest. [6]

Chapter 3

Family Background

Lancelot had been born on July 23, 1799, the fifth son and sixth child of William Dent (1762-1801) and Jane Wilkinson (1763-1840). Both families were Westmorland yeoman farmers, working land in the valley of the Lyvennet Beck between Shap Fell to the west and the market town of Appleby to the east. The southern end of the valley is enclosed by a high Fell that takes its name from the village of Crosby Ravensworth nestling beneath it. The church here contains monuments to numerous members of both families, while the graveyard is strewn with their tombstones. Higher up on the slopes towards Appleby is the farm called 'Trainlands'. **[Plate 51]** The modest farmhouse is a typical Westmorland 'longhouse' and above the front door is a carved inscription 'R.D. & W.D. 1755', though this refers to an extension added about a century after the main part was built, making it the oldest of the surviving Dent properties and the one from which our story takes its roots. One mile north of Crosby Ravensworth lies the village of Maulds Meaburn, the heartland of the Wilkinson family. Here also is Flass House, a property bought by Lancelot's great-grandfather John Dent (1694-1781) in 1730 and later rebuilt in the 1840s into the fine Palladian style mansion that is now Grade II listed. **[Plate 52]**

It is hardly surprising in this somewhat remote and isolated community that the two families should intermarry on a number of occasions over the generations. [See Appendix C.] Lancelot's mother, Jane Wilkinson had herself been the daughter of such a dynastic union, when Mary Dent (1726-1746) had married her cousin Lancelot Wilkinson (ca.1706-1767) in 1746. Mary Dent had two younger brothers. One was Robert Dent (1731-1805) who started off as a schoolmaster but was 'talent spotted' by a wealthy gentleman from London and invited down to join a banking firm in the City, Child & Co. – at that time bankers to the Royal family – later becoming a partner in the business. His son, John Dent (1761-1826) followed him into the partnership in 1795 by which time he was already an active Member of Parliament. **[Plate 49]** He is best known to history as 'Dog Dent', having promoted the Bill in 1796 that led to dog licences being introduced. He was offered a Baronetcy by William Pitt (the younger) in 1805, which he declined – a decision he later regretted – and his final years were blighted by stabbing pains in the face, a condition known as *tic doloureux* or *trigeminal neuralgia* that finally drove him to try and commit suicide.

Mary Dent's other brother was called William Dent (1740-1823) and he was the first member of either family to become involved with the East India Company, making himself extremely wealthy while working as a 'principal managing owner' of East Indiaman ships. These he bought and then syndicated 1/16th shares to investors that included his brother and clients of Child & Co. He never married though he appears to have had an illegitimate daughter, Mary Dent (1770-1867), to whom he left his large house in Wandsworth for her lifetime. His nephew Thomas Wilkinson (1759-1840) only received £100 from his uncle's will and went out to India to work for the East India Company Civil Service, becoming a provisional member of the Council of Bombay and a partner in the firm of Rivett, Wilkinson and Torin, which played a major role in the British annexation of the Malabar Coast. And he developed some business interests in China. These increased his self-made fortune several times over and on his return to England in the late 1790s he bought the lease of the elegant London property at 8 Fitzroy Square, plus his late brother-in-law's much extended farm at Trainlands. But he never married either, and in his later life he provided further financial support for his sister Jane and for the upbringing and education of her seven children – including Lancelot.

This quick and rather convoluted canter through Lancelot's ancestry on both the Dent and Wilkinson sides is designed to give readers some background to the influences that shaped his earlier life. How his family had emerged from yeoman farming stock to substantial wealth. How by the age of 20 he had been well educated, how he had close relatives who held influential positions in London, both in Parliament, banking and with the East India Company, and how these connections extended to the Indian Civil Service and trade with China. With this background it is not surprising that Lancelot and his five brothers all embarked on careers with a strong accent on India and the Far East. All, in different ways, showed drive and initiative, providing a powerful family network for mutual advancement. But while his brothers adopted careers in banking, commerce and civil administration, Lancelot would be the one who took the most active line in the opium trade. It was a very high risk game indeed. Ships that carried opium in one direction and silver in the other across the Bay of Bengal and the South China Sea had to face dangers from pirates, bad weather and the possibility of shipwreck. Men would be killed and, as we will see shortly, Lancelot himself would find himself in a situation where his life was under serious threat. His brothers would play key roles in how his own career developed and what follows is a brief sketch of the lives of each one. (His eldest sibling was in fact a sister called Elizabeth Dent (1797-1852) who remained a spinster throughout her life.)

Lancelot's eldest brother was Robert Dent (1793-1835) who in 1820, aged 26, became the junior partner in the firm of Rickards, Mackintosh, Law & Co. **[Plate 53]** This was a 'house of East India, China and General Agency' with London offices at 15 Bishopsgate, while the Mackintosh arm was based in Calcutta. [7] (Sometime after 1838 it went spectacularly bankrupt for £2½ million.) The partnership initially cost him £40,000, money that he may well have already earned working for the firm as a 'country trader' into Canton from the Portuguese enclave in Macau. It was probably in this small, close-knit community of Europeans that he first met Charlotte, the wife of James Thomas Robarts, who was the second most senior representative there for the East India Co. While still a junior EIC *supercargo,* James Robarts had set up his own company, Baring & Co., to trade in opium and cotton but was later forced to sell out to W.S. Davidson. James Robarts died in Macau on January 28, 1825, and just under 2 years later his widow married Robert Dent ('late of China') at St Pancras Old Church in London on November 9, 1826. Now living at Mitcham in south London, they would have four children (who survived infancy) over the years between 1828 and 1834. Robert continued as a working partner with Rickards, but he also undertook a wild speculation in South America when he bought the vast Aroa Estate in Venezuala. This had been owned by Simon Bolivar, the heroic liberator of much of the region from Spanish rule, and came onto the market after his death in 1830. Robert persuaded his uncle Thomas Wilkinson to share the £100,000 outlay with him. The estate was rich in copper mines and Robert even built a copper-smelting works at Ravenhead in St Helens, Lancashire to process the exported ore. Robert died in 1835 deeply in debt to his uncle who adopted his Aroa shares and the refinery, leaving them on his own death in 1840 to his spinster niece Elizabeth Dent. She only survived for another seven years and for some reason she left her considerable estate to her youngest brother, Wilkinson Dent. This led later to a furious family row with Robert Dent's children – and an expensive court-case – but while they argued, the Venezualan Government confiscated all foreign owned property and the shares became worthless.

John Dent (1795-1845) was Lancelot's next elder brother. **[Plate 54]** Educated at the East India Company's school at Haileybury, he went out to Calcutta as a writer for the company at the age of 17. After roles as an assistant to the Collector of Malabar and Malayalum Translator [8] to the Government, he was appointed as Deputy Collector of Sea Customs at Madras and Secretary to the Mint Committee. From 1824 to 1827 he was Secretary to the Madras Board of Trade. He had made a supposedly 'good marriage' in 1816 to Emily Ricketts the young daughter of the

Registrar of the Supreme Court of Judicature, Gilbert Ricketts, who was himself the younger brother of a Baronet. John and Emily lived for ten years in the province of Masulipatam and then in Arcot on the Coramandel Coast, returning to Madras in 1838 when he was appointed Head of the Board of Revenue for the whole Presidency. By this time they had nine children that survived infancy, their eldest son, born in 1820, being named after his father. John Dent Jnr. went to work with his uncle Lancelot in China and will become a key figure in the later story of the family and the founding of Hong Kong.

Lancelot's next brother was Thomas Dent (1796-1872) and his importance to the story lies mainly in the fact that he was the founder of the firm of Dent & Co., second of the two great 'Hong' businesses beside that of William Jardine and James Matheson, and one that would later become a founding member of the committee that established the Hong Kong and Shanghai Banking Corporation. **[Plate 55]** Thomas was educated at a school in Finchley, London, followed by a single year at Christ's College, Cambridge in 1815-16, and he was in Canton by 1817. Dent & Co. traced its origins to a Scotsman living in Macau called Walter Stephenson Davidson, who had become a naturalised Portuguese to circumvent the monopoly restrictions imposed by the East India Co. Walter Davidson acted as agent for George Baring, a member of the banking family, who had been an associate of James Robarts, the man whose widow Charlotte married Robert Dent in 1825. In 1824 Thomas Dent bought out Walter Davidson, changed the name to Dent & Co. and at the same time set up another partnership with Palmer & Co, the long-established trading company in Calcutta.

Next in the sequence of Lancelot's brothers was William Dent (1798-1877). **[Plate 56]** His schooling took place at Winchester before following the now established family tradition of going to Haileybury where he won the Bengali Prize. This prestigious honour had been awarded to his first cousin William Wilkinson the year before; already close friends from their shared boyhood in Westmorland, they sailed for India together in 1814 to become writers in the Bengal Civil Service. Their future careers would follow very similar paths, dedicated to roles of tax collection and dispensing justice in the district of Orissa, a region of EIC administration to the south of Calcutta. William Dent married young, which may not have helped his early career prospects, choosing as his bride the equally youthful Eliza Beaver in 1821. Tragedy struck only four years later when she died in childbirth, their two children also dying young. William now moved away from this region of sad memories and was promoted to be the superintendent for salt duties in Behar and later, more significantly, officiating agent for opium at Patna. (He married again, a Canadian called Mary Heffner, during a furlough to Europe in 1828 and had three further children.)

The last of Lancelot's brothers and the youngest by 15 months was Wilkinson Dent (1800-1886). **[Plate 58]** Their careers on the China coast would be closely linked throughout their whole lives, and while Lancelot remained primarily a trader, Wilkinson concentrated on the commercial side of Dent & Co. and stayed out in China longer than all the others, not finally returning to England for good until 1852. Of all the brothers, they were the only two who never married. When they first arrived in China in their early twenties, to join their elder brother Thomas, the trading rules laid down by the Chinese, the 'Eight Regulations', meant that they would live at Canton, not in the teeming city itself but in the rather weird, claustrophobic, men-only community of the 'factories', known to the Chinese as 'Faqi-city'.

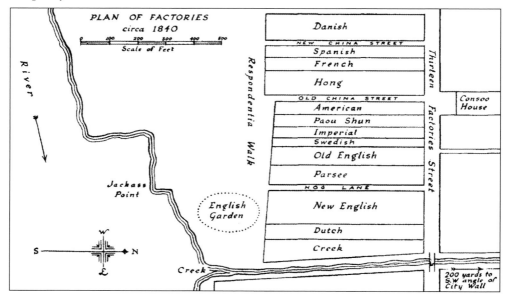

Map 5. Sketch map of the 'factories' at Canton, the area outside the walls of the city known as Faqi-city.

Chapter 4

Faqi-city

The administration of the city of Canton itself was in the hands of a Chinese Viceroy, appointed by the Emperor, who surrounded himself with a coterie of mandarins responsible for the civil administration of the city and its military defences. These consisted of the massive walls of the old city together with a number of forts along the banks of the Pearl River; a deterrent to pirates perhaps but worth little more when put to a serious challenge. The wealth of the city was generated by the guild of 13 merchants, the 'Co-Hong', who dealt directly with their foreign counterparts, the 'Hong'. Heading this first, select group was the 'thin-faced, wizened, frail, ascetic looking' [9] Howqua, who in 1834 was estimated to be worth £4½ million, [10] while at his death in 1843 his wealth was ten times greater than that of Nathan Rothschild. [11] The source of his great wealth lay in his family's large tea estates in the Bohea region and, unlike his fellow members of the Co-Hong such as Moqua and Gowqua who were bon-vivants of jovial disposition, he led a life of austere simplicity, which matched his reputation for rigid honesty and, at times, remarkable generosity.

The two groups of traders understood each other perfectly well through a common commercial language of supply and demand, of bargaining and barter. They recognised the need to pay commissions to lubricate a final deal, signed off and sealed with a 'chop' in the Consoo House, the Co-Hong's equivalent of a Chamber of Commerce. It was also tacitly understood that, where necessary, bribes had to be paid to non-commercial mandarins – and the Viceroy. Each group held the other in mutual, cordial respect with copious amounts of reciprocal entertainment.

The foreign community at Canton lived in the enclave, 'Faqi-city', outside the city walls to the south-west. It extended along the waterfront for about 350 yards between Jackass Point to the west, via the 'English Garden', to 'the Creek' at the eastern extremity. The various factories were set back about 50 yards from the bank of the river, the open space in front being known officially as Respondentia Walk but referred to as the *maidan*. [See Map 5] The frontage of each factory was quite narrow but they extended back nearly 200 yards to provide a warren of warehouses, living accommodation and offices, with open courtyards and entertainment rooms. In front of each factory stood a flag-pole to display a national ensign or a house-flag. **[Plate 50]** Between the factories ran two crowded streets named 'Hog Lane' and 'Old China Street' where the Chinese set up market-stalls selling meat, fish, rice, vegetables and fruit, together with timber, furniture and other goods that would be available in a normal town. The risk of fire was always present and the factories had all been effectively rebuilt after the 'Great Fire' of 1822. Another fire threatened in 1835, after two years in which the factories had also been damaged by flood-waters. [12]

Up to 1834 the largest factory, the 'Imperial', belonged to the East India Company, where the British traders in Canton were supervised by the President of a Select Committee of that company. This grand building with its branching staircase had a dining-room 'of vast proportions', along with an extensive library and a billiard room. It became the equivalent of an officers' mess for the British community, the largest national component. In 1834 this consisted of 66 traders and their staff; by 1837, the number had risen to over 150. The second largest factory was that of the Parsee merchants while others were occupied by traders from the United States, led by Russell & Co, and other representatives from France and Holland. The Swedish, Austrian, Spanish and Danish merchants had all left by 1834 and Jardine, Matheson took over vacated premises nearest the Creek, a muddy inlet that separated the foreign enclave from the old city. William Jardine had somehow managed to get himself appointed as the Danish consul, so the flag of that country flew on the flag-pole and he was later succeeded in this role by his partner James Matheson. Hollingworth Magniac was the consular representative for Prussia while Thomas Dent held that post, unlikely as it may seem, for Sardinia. Consular officers enjoyed the privilege of being allowed communication privileges with the city mandarins and it is important to understand that Great Britain had no such representative in any, however minor, ambassadorial role. Being a consul had another advantage; it enabled the titleholder, where expedient, to escape complying with the rules laid down by the EIC.

The all-male residents of 'Faqi-city' were forbidden to penetrate outside the enclave on the landward side, every access road being guarded by Chinese police posts. Each factory had its own jetty for loading and unloading cargo and in between these was a whole floating community of Chinese sampans and ferries, together with the 'flower-boats' of the local prostitutes. Contact with these was strongly discouraged, by the British at least, though less notice was taken of visits to the 'girlie' craft at Whampoa. Playing whist, dining and drinking were the prime sources of evening entertainment. The East India Co. had installed a piano and after dinner it was not uncommon for the men to dance together into the small hours. Few went to bed sober.

It was a claustrophobic existence. [13] Exercise was restricted to strolling up and down the *maidan*, though the British had formed a Regatta Club, using a small fleet of sailing yachts commissioned from a local boat-builder. There were also rowing races between six-oared gigs and once a season there were longer races down the Pearl River. One year, in appalling weather, the Dent's contender over the 25-mile course was the yacht *Gypsy*, Jardine's was called *Thistle*, and the fact that *Gypsy* won in a time of 4 hours merely intensified the rivalry between these two ambitious and highly competitive houses. [14]

Chapter 5

The Rivals

As international competition increased in the 1820s, so the British Government realised that the EIC's remaining monopoly powers were restricting the country's trading opportunities and in 1833 it brought in the Government of India Act (the Charter Act) that divested the company of all its exporting activities. At the same time they took over direct control of operations with China by the appointment of a 'Superintendent for Trade'. The implications of this move, with its far-reaching consequences, will be recounted in the following chapter, but for now we should review the state of trade at the time and the roles of the leading actors in the unfolding drama of opium.

By 1834 the imports of opium into China, from all countries and all trading agents, had reached the staggering figure of 30,000 chests per annum, and it was the British that commanded the major share. (21,250 chests, valued at $14 million.) And some traders, like James Innes, were ignoring the Regulations completely, bypassing Canton and trading directly from Macau up the east coast of China into ports and harbours such as Amoy, Swatow and Fuzhou.

British trading interests became dominated by the two rival partnerships – Jardine, Matheson & Co, the self-styled 'Princely House', and Dent & Co., the 'Precious and Compliant Company'. Both had become wealthy by working purely on commission; now the changed environment meant that they could trade as principals in both the import and export of all types of goods and commodities.

The stakes were raised considerably, along with the associated risks. Both firms had links with existing agencies in Calcutta and Bombay but they now needed sources of finance in London. Thomas Dent had been head of the Dent operations in Canton since 1817 and he returned to England as a very wealthy man in 1833, leaving his brother Lancelot in charge of the trade in China, together with the youngest brother Wilkinson Dent. Back in London Thomas Dent developed the family interest in the merchant banking business of Rickards, Mackintosh & Co. This later joined up with another firm to become Dent, Palmer & Co. while Thomas also started a new merchant banking business trading under the name of Thomas Dent & Co., describing themselves as 'East India and Commission Agents'. He also forged close links with a governor of the Bank of England, the impressive Horsley Palmer, and even entertained ambitions, never to be realised, of becoming a director of the Bank himself.

Jardine, Matheson had been founded in 1832 with eight partners of whom William Jardine was the senior. Born in 1784, he was the second son of a Scottish farming family from Dumfries, studied medicine at the Royal College of Surgeons in Edinburgh and spent the years between 1802 and 1817 as a ship's surgeon on a number of vessels owned by the East India Co. trading in the Far East. The company allowed their officers, known in this capacity as *supercargoes*, to take certain amounts of cargo for trading on their own behalf and William Jardine soon discovered that he had a considerable talent in this sphere, and that the most profitable commodity was opium. He described it as 'the safest and most gentlemanlike speculation I am aware of'. He also established a close friendship with the 26 year old Charles Magniac who was supervising his father's watch business at Canton. In 1817 William Jardine gave up his peripatetic life on board ship and became an independent commission trader for agencies like the Parsee firm owned by Jamsetjee Jejeebhoy, who, incidentally, would later become the first Indian to be knighted by Queen Victoria.

James Matheson arrived in Canton twelve months later, having originally gone out to Calcutta where his father had started a trading operation. He was 12 years younger than William Jardine and also the second son of a Scottish family, this time from Lairg in Sutherland and, again like William Jardine, he had been educated in Edinburgh University. With such similar backgrounds it is hardly surprising that they soon struck up a close association. James Matheson's first role in Canton had been as a partner in a Spanish trading house and because Spain had some concessions at the port of Amoy that had fallen into disuse, he was the first European to test the market there on board a ship flying the Spanish flag. He managed to dispose of opium worth £33,000 and could report back that the potential for this traffic was immense. So William Jardine invited him into partnership, a partnership to which Matheson could contribute useful capital of £20,000. [15]

At the beginning of 1834 the largest trading house at Canton was Magniacs, which already had a strong banking operation in London. But the Canton end ran into a management crisis on the death of Charles Magniac that year. Charles had two brothers, Hollingworth and Daniel, and when Hollingworth assumed the reins of the company his first action was to sack Daniel for the reprehensible 'sin' of marrying his Chinese mistress. He himself wished to retire back to England, though he was prepared to leave his capital in the partnership, so he was in urgent need of recruiting new partners or merging it with another. The partnership he chose was that of Jardine and Matheson.

The characters of the leading players in the two rival partnerships were very different. William Jardine was generous, extrovert and sociable, with a great capacity for making friends combined with an even greater capacity for hard work. He deplored time-wasters and was famous for not having any chairs in his office, standing up to work at his own desk and ensuring that visitors were not encouraged to linger. The Chinese called him the 'iron-headed rat', a reference to a skirmish with Chinese police in which he had been hit over the head by a heavy club – without apparently incurring any injury. Harriet Low, who described herself as the 'travelling spinster of Macau', enjoyed his company, referring to him as 'the great man of Canton', though mainly, she implied, on the basis that 'he was rich'. [16] He was also very political, with Whig sympathies, and realised that trade with China could not be expanded without some form of pressure being applied by the British Government to break down the intransigence of the Imperial Court. If diplomacy failed, he was already contemplating a resort to more forceful methods.

There are virtually no pen-portraits of Lancelot Dent and none of his personal correspondence survives, so his character has to be built up from his actions, his responses to crises and what is known of his business dealings. He had been out in Canton with his elder brother Thomas since about 1825-6, though a document dated July 7, 1824, shows that he had originally borrowed money from his brother Robert Dent to buy into the Keir partnership, Madeira wine merchants. [17] It seems that he was a man of concise speech, stubborn and obstinate when he had to be and not a particularly easy socialiser, though a biographer claimed that 'his large-mindedness and affability' made him more popular than his brother Thomas Dent.[18] Members of the Co-Hong believed him to be a 'very soft-hearted man'. [19] Like William Jardine, he had a reputation for straight dealing and keeping his word, once a deal had been struck, in Lancelot's case 'combined with an unusual attention to detail, bordering on pedantry'. Politically he was a Tory sympathiser, having 'a practical recognition that coercive measures against the Chinese to expand trading opportunities could be counter-productive'. In 1836, for example, he founded and endowed the Morrison Education Society with the object of 'fostering greater mutual understanding between Chinese and Western cultures'. He had always been a great admirer of the way the EIC had conducted its business and thought that William Jardine's 'hawkish' approach might be counter-productive.

Rivalry between the two firms was intense and not always cordial. Some of it probably went back to historical mistrust between the English Borderers and their

Scottish counterparts. (as related in Book 1) In the days of the EIC, the President of the Select Committee, who despised all private traders, described the Dents as the 'more respectable' part of the British community while railing against Jardine for allowing Capt. Innes to break one of the 'Eight Regulations' by trading directly up the coast. Robert Inglis, a senior writer for Jardine, Matheson, left that organisation and joined Dents, though whether he was bribed away or moved of his own free will is not known.

The role of the EIC's Select Committee was taken over in 1834 by the establishment of a British Chamber of Commerce, the founding of which had not been without its problems and its 'usefulness was negated by the petty jealousies of the community'. [20] James Matheson, chosen as the first chairman when the Dent contingent refused to turn up for the election meeting, wrote later that 'some had an expectation that it would tend to counteract the influence of our House.' This was the first of many public clashes between the two great Hongs, a rivalry that would continue for the next 50 years. Jardines had started a newspaper, the *Canton Register* in 1828; Dents immediately responded by printing their own paper called the *Canton Press*. 'The tone of each paper was soon lowered by scurrilous attacks on the other.' [21] At one point the rival editors challenged each other to a duel and this was only thwarted 'by the common sense of the community'.

Both partnerships designed and sponsored the construction of their own fleets of 'opium clippers'. The classic ships of the EIC, the 'East Indiamen', had been large, slow and bulky, typically of between 600-800 tons and they took between two and three months to sail between India and China. The clippers were smaller, sleeker and much faster, capable of beating their way up through the north-east monsoon, though with their vast heads of canvas they needed skilful handling and their legendary captains were paid very handsomely indeed. In the days of the EIC only one transit from Calcutta to Canton was possible per season; the clippers could manage three. By 1838, Jardine, Matheson had a total fleet of twelve ships, of which clippers accounted for four; [22] Dent & Co. had the same number. [23] The pride of the Jardine fleet was the *Red Rover*, while Dents' was *Waterwitch*, and neither would yield to the other as to which was the fastest or best. **[Plate 63]** When William Jardine sent some of his clippers to trade with the coastal communities at places like Amoy, Chimo Bay and Fuzhow, Lancelot Dent ordered his captains to moor close-by and offer opium at lower prices. This crippling price war was bad for both houses and they soon came to an agreement to control prices on the coastal trade at a level that was profitable to them both yet deterred smaller competitors trying to cash in on this market.

Then there was the increasingly important question of insurance. The Canton Insurance Cooperative was initially started as a joint business between the two houses, the management responsibility alternating every five years, but after 1835 they split, Jardines operating as the Canton Insurance Ltd. and Dents as the Union Insurance Co. of Canton. They also clashed on the delicate matter of precedence, neither being prepared to place their signature on any document below that of the other, meaning that all such paperwork had to be prepared in duplicate.

One of the most interesting and colourful characters on the China coast was the missionary Karl (Charles) Gutzlaff. Born in Pomerania in 1803, he became a Protestant missionary and had been initially sent to Java in the Dutch East Indies by the Netherlands Missionary Society in 1828. He learnt Chinese, wore Chinese clothes and adopted the Chinese name of Pinyin. He was persuaded by William Jardine to accompany his early attempts to open up trade in some of the ports up the East coast of China. In October 1832, William Jardine had written a letter to him that included the following: 'Though it is our earnest wish that you should not in any way injure the grand object you have in view by appearing interested in what by many is considered an immoral traffic ...... you must be well aware that no other cargo holds out a prospect of gain sufficient to engage in such an expensive expedition. Opium appears to be the only article able to gratify the cupidity of the authorities on the coast.' [24] Gutzlaff's main role was to act as an interpreter, engaging with the local mandarins to persuade them that the mission was entirely friendly, bringing enlightenment to those who would listen and prosperity to those who wished to trade. The printing of the religious tracts that he distributed were paid for by William Jardine and he only suffered minor qualms from his dichotomous situation, dispensing Christian literature with one hand while lubricating the sale of opium with the other. As he noted in his journal; 'After much consultation with others and a conflict in my own mind, I embarked on the *Sylph* on October 20th, 1832.' [25] These voyages produced not only profits for Jardines but also served the commendable role of conducting surveys of navigable channels, reefs and sandbanks. And these formed the basis of charts that would be used for the next hundred years or more.

Gutzlaff also developed a clever philosophical argument to counter the Chinese obstinacy about changing their attitudes to foreign influences, an obduracy that hid behind the statement that things must not change because the 'old laws were immutable'. Yet in the 'old days' foreign travellers had been made welcome. Furthermore, the 'old laws' said nothing about the 'Eight Regulations' nor the rulings against the import of opium, so these had no justification – and could therefore be disregarded. It would prove to be a useful argument for those who would later urge the use of military action to release the Chinese people from their bondage of superstition and outdated ways of thinking. [26]

Chapter 6

Overture to Conflict

As mentioned at the start of the previous chapter, in 1833 the British Government appointed their first 'Superintendent of Trade' in China. This appointment by the Foreign Office was as a representative of the King himself, and therefore, in spite of the title, his role would be a diplomatic one, rather than commercial. The first of these Superintendents was Lord Napier, a Captain in the Royal Navy, variously described as a 'tall, raw Scotsman with light hair' and 'a humourless Scot with little knowledge of Eastern affairs, whose main interests were the Royal Navy and sheep farming.' [27] He arrived in July 1834 and took up residence with his wife, his staff and his chaplain in Macau. A week later he proceeded with his retinue up to Canton and announced his arrival by writing to the Viceroy of Canton, in terms of equality as a 'Plenipotentiary', a normal procedure in European diplomacy.

This caused the deepest offense. The Emperor demanded that any consular approach by a 'barbarian eye' had to be accompanied by 'kow-towing tribute' at the Celestial Court first – as Lords Macartney and Amherst had both discovered on earlier occasions – and Lord Napier had tried to bypass this protocol yet again. Had the Viceroy accepted the letter, he would have reversed a policy that had been in place for 1,500 years. A month of negotiations with the mandarins failed to resolve the deadlock, and although Lord Napier told the British community that he was minded to return to Macau to await further instructions from London, the enraged Viceroy took matters into his own hands. He blockaded the foreign community by placing an assembly of troops on the *maidan*, stopped all trade, withdrew all native servants, and refused the sale of food to foreigners until Lord Napier departed.

His Lordship interpreted this as an Act of War and ordered two frigates to come up to Canton, though his orders were that they should only open fire if shot at first. They reached the anchorage at Whampoa five days later after their passage had been somewhat ineffectually disputed at the Bogue forts. But then Lord Napier was struck down by a fever and, when told his life was in danger if he did not get medical treatment soon, he effectively capitulated and ordered the frigates away in return for an offer of safe-passage in another vessel. Even so, the Chinese held him up for five days and trumpeted a great naval victory, claiming that they had driven off the frigates by superior force of arms. Lord Napier died immediately after his arrival at Macao but the seeds of a military intervention had been sown.

To pursue his political line, William Jardine sent James Matheson to accompany Lord Napier's widow back to London and try and explain the reality of the situation to the Foreign Office. His objectives were twofold; to educate them on the Chinese mindset and to convince them that any policy on 'Free Trade' could not succeed in Canton without the backing of naval strength. James Matheson did manage to have a meeting with the then Foreign Secretary, the Duke of Wellington, at which he presented a Petition to King William IV, signed by sixty four British merchants, urging that a powerful naval force should be sent. But the meeting did not go well, and Matheson reported back in a letter to William Jardine that he had had to try and deal with 'a cold-blooded fellow ... a strenuous advocate for submissiveness and servility'. [28] Wellington's tenure at the Foreign Office was very brief and he was succeeded the following year by Lord Palmerston. In another letter James Matheson wrote; [29]

> The fact is, Jardine, people here appear to be so comfortable in this magnificent country, so entirely satisfied in all their desires, that so long as domestic affairs, including markets, go right, they cannot really be brought to think of us outlanders. Until therefore there is a stoppage of trade, or something to touch the pockets of the merchants and ship-owners, expect no sympathy here. The more successful you are in keeping things quiet, no matter at what sacrifice or in what manner, the less sympathy you will have here. Lord Palmerston means to do nothing.

The implications of the 'Napier incident' were threefold. The Chinese became emboldened to continue to treat foreigners with utter disdain while also beginning to invest in improvements to their fortifications, particularly at the Bogue. There they seized an officer off the Jardine brig *Fairy Queen*, put him in irons and demanded a $500 ransom. Secondly, the Foreign Office began to realise that their next representative might even spark an armed conflict, one for which the country was completely unprepared both politically and in terms of sheer logistics. Palmerston himself did take a very different attitude to that of his predecessor, seeing the mantra of 'Free Trade' as a vital part of his plans for Imperial expansion, but timing was crucial. The public, through the House of Commons, had to be won over, but first of all the right man had to be appointed as the new Superintendent of Trade. Thirdly, the British community in Canton found themselves in many ways worse off than before, having lost the prestige of the East India Company and not gained a robust defender of their interests in substitution.

A most revealing letter was sent under the seal of Dent & Co., doubtless dictated by Lancelot Dent, to Baring & Co., their London correspondents at the time, dated April 1, 1835. [30] (It was not received until Sept 24, which highlights the time-lag in the receipt of news and the issuing of instructions.)

> At the close of the first shipping season since the termination of the Company's Charter, we are induced to address you more fully than in our usual commercial circulars. By the opening of the trade to China, a great change took place in the mode of conducting the business of this Port; a change which to many was the grounds of the most sanguine hope, to others of danger to its continuation, and to all a matter of speculation. Under these circumstances it is a subject of congratulation, that if all the flattering results which were anticipated have not been realised, the general current of trade has proceeded on the whole prosperously and uninterruptedly – *with the exception of the discussion connected with the residence of H.M. Superintendent in Canton.* (Author's italics. Given the new attitude shown by the Chinese, this phrase is a rather charming understatement.)

The letter, consisting of 18 large pages, then goes into detailed statistics of trade over the previous five years, information previously kept confidential by the EIC. There is a breakdown of all classes of imports (totalling $26,295,592 in 1833-4), covering woollens, cotton goods and raw fibre, metals – mainly from America – and, of course, opium, which accounted for the bulk at $14,006,605. (But average prices per chest had fallen over the past five years, from $950 to $650.) There are informative notes about each category; British manufactured broadcloth had suffered from an oversupply with 'all spirit of speculation being checked by the apprehended glut'; bandana handkerchiefs were much sought after, particularly 'scarlet Monteiths', while 'only chintzes of good quality and patterns have been in demand'. Exports for the year had amounted to $23,442,639, of which bullion from opium sales had represented 40%. 'A much greater quantity of tea – 42,809,400lbs – has been shipped to England than in any former year .... chiefly in those descriptions which are usually exported to America and the Continent of Europe.' This figure is then broken down into 15 grades, each with average unit prices, ranging from the expensive Hysons and Gunpowders, through the Pekoes and Twankeys to the cheaper Congous and Boheas, which together accounted for 72%. 'The consumption of raw silk from the manufacturers in England has greatly increased .... and we may look forward to its becoming a still more important feature in exports from China,' though the 'consumption in England of Nankeen cloth appears to be nearly extinct.'

The man Palmerston chose as the next 'Plenipotentiary of Trade' was another naval officer, Captain Charles Elliot, once characterised as 'a nervous, headstrong man with a fatal sense of his own importance.' [31] He had been born in 1801 and joined the Royal Navy as a midshipman in 1815. He saw service against pirates in the Mediterranean, then in the East Indies and finally the West Indies. There he married Clara Windsor in 1828. Retiring from active service with the rank of Captain, he joined the Foreign Office and was sent on a three year posting to Guiana in 1830, his post being 'Protector of Slaves' and a member of the Court of Policy. Here he showed his skills both as a diplomatic official in a largely policing role and as a communicator with his masters back in London, where his reports were influential in the Government's drafting of the Slavery Abolition Act of 1833. The Governor of Guiana wrote to the Treasury in glowing terms, praising Elliot not only for 'the zealous and efficient execution of the duties of his office' but also for the fact that he 'contributed far beyond what the functions of his particular office required of him.' [32]

His next posting was to China where he arrived as a member of the unfortunate Lord Napier's staff, being responsible for the regulation of British shipping between Macau and Canton. Ships on legitimate trade were permitted to sail up the Pearl River as far as the last deep water anchorage at Whampoa, about 14 miles from Canton, from where transhipments of both imports and exports were made via Chinese junks. Most inbound shipments of opium were offloaded into 'receiving ships', the hulks of obsolete merchantmen, at Lintin, an island anchorage between Macao and the Bocca Tigris narrows. From these the Chinese merchants offloaded their purchases into 'fast boats' propelled by crews of 16 or 20 rowers which then delivered the chests to their distribution points. This illicit trade was carried out mainly at night, though imposition of the rules against opium smuggling were so lax, at least up until 1838, that these craft might often be seen on their frantic missions by daylight. Some opium was even concealed among legitimate cargo and taken all the way up to Whampoa.

Elliot found his role somewhat frustrating, recording that he only had authority 'over the lawful trade, my Government not being acquainted with any other.' [33] He was naive if he really believed this, but it was the official stance. He also had a personal dilemma; morally he strongly disapproved of the opium trade yet many of the traders became his personal friends. Elliot had distinguished himself by his very British display of bravery during the action that took place when Lord Napier made his brief and unsuccessful show of strength. Accompanying the frigates 'HMS *Andromache*' and 'HMS *Imogene*' through the fire from the Bogue fort in a small cutter, he sat calmly at the tiller 'under a large umbrella to protect himself from the broiling sun.' [34]

After Lord Napier's death in 1834, the role of 'Superintendent of Trade' had passed successively to a Mr John Davis and then Sir George Robinson, who sat in their offices in Macau merely signing the necessary paperwork to maintain the flow of trade. In Canton, their health was sarcastically drunk with a toast to 'them that's awa'. When Palmerston promoted Captain Elliot to the role in 1836, the British merchants were probably delighted that now at last their interests were going to be championed and protected by a man of action. He had gained valuable experience of their situation, he knew them all as individuals and his personal bravery was beyond doubt. And presumably his new brief had the backing of promises of more robust support from the Foreign Office. Surely he would not make the same mistakes as his predecessors.

He seemed to start well. Without waiting for any licence, he sailed straight up to Canton, raised the British flag on the flagpole outside the old EIC building and then, as Palmerston had instructed him, submitted a petition to the Viceroy. This he believed was couched in more conciliatory terms than Lord Napier's, though the underlying request was the same; to be recognised as a representative of the Crown. This was summarily rejected. He would only be allowed to stay in Canton 'under the existing regulations applicable to chief supercargoes .... as a *Taipan*, and as the spokesperson for the merchants', a role already exercised by the chairman of the Chamber of Commerce. For a brief time he tried to petition through the mandarins but without success. Humiliated and frustrated, Elliot struck his flag and withdrew himself from Canton to rejoin his wife at Macau.

Lancelot wrote to his Dent partners in London on December 8, 1837, stating that the trade of Canton was generally proceeding without interruption, 'not withstanding the strict measures to prevent the introduction of opium.' [35] He went on to say that 'an edict has appeared threatening the stoppage of the whole foreign trade in a month unless the opium ships are sent away .... and Capt Elliot has found it necessary to leave Canton in consequence of some misunderstandings as to the mode of communication between himself and the local authorities.'

From Macau Elliot wrote to Lord Palmerston requesting a naval presence to back his authority and so the Foreign office despatched two frigates under Admiral Sir Charles Maitland. These anchored below the Bogue fort while Elliot returned to Canton to try and arrange an interview for the Admiral with the Viceroy. The latter's response was a total refusal, combined with an edict that all shipping on the river was to be searched in case Admiral Maitland was on board. Tensions mounted and in one incident the schooner *Bombay* was fired upon. Elliot took this as a 'public insult which ought to be resented', so he sailed at the head of the two frigates and demanded a meeting with the Chinese Admiral to extract an apology. Here he was presented with a letter claiming that the *Bombay* incident had never taken place; it had been a figment of someone's imagination. Face to face the Chinese Admiral remarked; 'I am a Commander as well as you and I can easily fancy what your feelings must have been on hearing such a report, but it is not true.' [36] Elliot, ever the conciliator, withdrew his ships and sailed back to Macao. William Jardine expressed his disgust and contempt in a note dated July 8, 1838; 'an English ship of the line against some Chinese junks?'

The only positive aspect of this fiasco was that Admiral Maitland could make an assessment of the construction and armaments in the Bogue forts. He was unimpressed and reported as such on his return to Calcutta.

In an almost exact repeat of Napier's humiliation three years earlier, Elliot's capitulation boosted the confidence of the Viceroy in Canton who now levied a new duty on all trade. This was ostensibly to pay for a heavy chain boom that could be erected across the Pearl River to control shipping movements more efficiently. This levy squeezed $100,000 out of the coffers of the Hong merchants. Further insults and humiliations were piled on the foreign community when the Viceroy ordered the conversion of the *maidan* into an execution ground, making it known that opium smugglers would be strangled there in public. Only his fellow countrymen at first, but with the implication that foreigners might be treated similarly in future.

There was a furious reaction in the foreign community, one that was fortunately endorsed by the mandarins and the Co-Hong merchants, who were as anxious as their counterparts to maintain the status quo. Soon the scaffold was dismantled and moved to the Chinese quarter. William Jardine's analysis of the hardening of the Viceroy's attitude was perceptive. 'He has received a severe reprimand from the Emperor for being too indolent with the opium dealers, brokers and smokers. In consequence he has been seizing, trying and strangling the poor devils without mercy. Three or four men are carried off daily by confinement and torture. They are timid fellows here and stand a good deal from their oppressive rulers.' Elliot tried to persuade the opium traders to show some respect for the regulations and at least not bring any opium upstream from Lintin, but his suggestions were ignored. One of the chief offenders was Captain James Innes who even used European seamen to man the schooners involved.

There had indeed been a hardening of attitude in Peking. The Emperor Daoguang was very different from his obese, bejewelled predecessor Jiaguin, being pinched and angular in appearance and thrifty and parsimonious in his outlook. On his accession to the Celestial Throne in 1820 he had halved the number of court entertainers to only 390 and reduced the kitchen staff to a mere 200. He deliberately wore rather shabby clothes. In 1836 there had been a major debate within the Court about how to deal with the opium situation; on one side were those arguing to make the trade legal and therefore subject to import duties and taxes like any other commodity, while the moralists pushed for complete prohibition. (These debates would be precisely echoed in the United States in 1919 during the run-up to the Volstead Act for alcohol suppression, and the 18th amendment to the American Constitution that followed.) If the Emperor was concerned about the effect of the widespread opium addiction on the morals of his subjects and their general productivity, he was even more concerned on what it was doing to the economy of the country. This was the tipping point. The trade imbalance had reached such a proportion that the reserves of bullion were being seriously depleted and inflation was rampant. Between 1800 and 1810, there had been a net inflow of wealth into the country of $26 million; in the decade between 1828 and 1838 this had swung round into a net deficit of $38 million. And the reason was entirely due to opium.

On July 10, 1838, the regional governor of the provinces of Hupei and Hunan, Lin Zexu, penned his opinion to the Emperor as follows; 'if we continue to pamper (the opium habit), a few decades from now we shall not only be without soldiers but also in want of silver to provide an army.' This view became the consensus and those in favour of a total ban on trade and consumption won the day. In truth though, it represented no change in official policy since the prohibition edict of 1799; the real problem was one of enforcement. Daoguang's first step was to issue an Imperial Edict that included the following;

> Since opium has spread its baneful influence through China, the quantity of silver exported has yearly been on the increase, till its price has become enhanced to such an extent that the copper coin has depreciated and the land and capitalisation taxes, the transport of grain and the gabel, all alike hampered. If steps be not taken for our defence ... the useful wealth of China will be poured into the fathomless abyss of transmarine regions.

His second step was to appoint an enforcer and the man he chose as his 'Commissioner' was Lin Zexu himself. This official was unique among his contemporaries for being not only efficient but utterly incorruptible. Appointed in December 1838, his brief from the Emperor was that he should 'exert all his strength to resolve this matter .... he must, according to the place and circumstances, radically sever the trunk from its roots.' Lin had already argued that the obvious solution was to treat foreign smugglers in exactly the same way as their Chinese counterparts. When the news of his appointment reached Canton in early January, William Jardine expressed his cynicism that things might change for a short time but that they would soon return to normal. He was wrong.

One cannot be sure whether William Jardine's decision in December 1838 to leave Canton was one of luck or shrewd judgement. Probably the latter, because he could calculate that Lin would target his opprobrium and condemnation on the man he saw as the figurehead of the opium smugglers in the foreign community. And this mantle would now fall on the shoulders of Lancelot Dent. William Jardine's last instruction to James Matheson was that all the opium held in the partners' receiving ship at Lintin should be distributed across their clipper fleet and sent up the coast with Captain Innes. William Jardine set sail for Macau and thence to London on January 30, and the night before there was a sumptuous banquet given at the Chamber of Commerce to send him on his way. 166 members of the foreign community sat down to dinner, each attended by their own servant. Endless toasts were drunk in his honour and speeches made to wish him success in his avowed purpose of returning to Scotland, finding a wife and founding a dynasty. In his reply, William Jardine joked that at his age, 54, he could only hope to attract a woman who was 'fair, fat and forty'. [37] The evening ended with William Jardine having a final dance with his friend Mr Wetmore.

The one person who did not attend was Lancelot Dent; he had never liked his great rival and could anticipate the problems that he would now have to contend with. But unlike William Jardine he was prepared to stand and stay and try to bluff his way out.

Chapter 7

The Siege of the Factories and an Incident at Chuanbi

Commissioner Lin was 55 years old, 'a large, stout man with a dignified air and harsh expression.' He arrived in Canton with his small group of assistants on March 10, 1839, and, as an example of his fastidiousness, it is claimed that he paid for all their travelling expenses out of his own pocket. He himself was a considerable scholar but had no experience of meeting foreigners, though he was shrewd enough to recognise that western science would repay study. Included in his coterie were four interpreters who had been educated in missionary schools overseas, and he set them to work translating English textbooks and extracts from the local newspapers.

Two days before Lin's arrival, Lancelot Dent had anticipated the event in a letter to his London partners. [38] 'The course he (Lin) may see fit to pursue in carrying the object of his mission into effect must have some important bearing on the present state of the Foreign Commerce ... you and all parties interested in the valuable trade to this country will learn with regret the highly unsatisfactory and very precarious state of our relations with the Chinese Government; a position from which it will require extreme caution and great tact to extricate us without endangering the trade generally. A memorial to the British Parliament from HM subjects in China is just now in contemplation.' Immediately before this letter was sent, a hasty postscript was added to say that he had ordered Dent & Co.'s treasury to close for all transactions.

Lin's first move was to issue an edict that all opium stocks held in China, whether in warehouses or on board receiving ships, were to be handed over forthwith. In addition, he demanded that everyone in any way associated with the opium trade must leave China and sign a bond stating that, should they return, their lives would be forfeited.

Matters now moved quickly. On March 18 Lin ordered all trade to be frozen. He then held a meeting with the Chinese merchants of the 'Co-Hong' and had two of their most senior representatives, Howqua and Mowqua, escorted down to the foreign factories wearing wooden yokes chained around their necks, like portable pillories, a degrading punishment normally reserved for petty thieves. Howqua pleaded with the Hong merchants to obey Lin's instructions to the letter, otherwise they would be executed and so would the other members of the Co-Hong in quick succession. In a letter to William Jardine, James Matheson described the incident as 'the most complete exhibition of humbug ever witnessed in China'. He had yet to grasp Lin's steely resolution.

Lin then ordered that Lancelot Dent should come to see him in person at the Conshoo House on March 22. At a hastily convened meeting in the Chamber of Commerce, his compatriots urged him to agree and initially, according to one writer, 'everything chivalrous in Mr Dent's nature prompted him to comply.' [39] But on reflection Lancelot told them that this would be a sign of weakness and that they should stall for time. His younger brother, Wilkinson Dent, told the gathering; 'if you let him go, I will lay his death at your door!' Lancelot sent a reply to Lin stating that he needed a day or two to consider the position and anyway the 22nd was a Sunday when he would be attending church. He also demanded an assurance of safe conduct while at the same time offering to give up 1,037 chests of opium. This sort of sop had always worked in the past.

Meanwhile Elliot had been kept informed of the deteriorating situation and he ordered all ships at Macau and Lintin to leave and rally in the deep water anchorage off the island of Hong Kong, under the protection of the Royal Navy sloop HMS *Larne*. There they were to raise their national flags and be prepared to resist any action by the Chinese navy. He himself boarded his armed cutter, the *Louisa*, and through a combination of skilful handling of his boat and a favourable breeze he managed to slip past the blockading war-junks. Four miles from his destination, he donned his full naval uniform and transferred to an unarmed gig rowed by four sailors. At 6 pm on the evening of March 24 he stepped onto the jetty outside the British factory, in cocked-hat and epaulettes and with his sword at his side, and ordered the Union Jack to be raised on the flagpole. 'There is,' he declared, 'a sense of support in the sight of that honoured flag, fly where it will.' [40] Then, in a bravado gesture of defiance, he announced that he was taking Lancelot Dent under his personal protection and moved him into his own private quarters. He dashed off a succession of letters to Lord Palmerston. 'It was my resolution to reach these factories or sacrifice my own life.' He avowed to resist 'aggression against foreign persons and property ..... this is my capital duty as a Queen's officer.' In his previous encounters with Lancelot Dent, he had found him a diplomatic embarrassment; now he became 'one of our most respected merchants in Canton.' [41]

Elliot's action triggered what came to be known as 'the siege of the factories'. Lin ordered all Chinese staff and servants to leave, food supplies to be banned and dire penalties imposed for any breach of his orders. Agitators were positively encouraged to demonstrate on the *maidan*, while the local police turned a blind eye as an armed mob started smashing in the doors and windows on the facade of the Chamber of Commerce. In retrospect it is remarkable that no shots were fired. The foreign community found themselves thrown onto their own resources, raiding their own trading stocks to provide makeshift meals. Clerks became cooks, while *compradors,* more used to keeping accounts, had to learn how to do laundry work.

Lin then changed tack and stated that he no longer wished to arrest Lancelot Dent but that he now held Elliot himself personally responsible for 'speedily arranging the delivery of the opium and the giving of bonds.' [42] One week later Elliot effectively capitulated, sending a message to Lin committing himself to deliver up all the opium stocks held anywhere on the Pearl River, an amount he calculated, without any accurate input from the merchants themselves, as being precisely 20, 236 chests. But he had failed to take into account those that James Matheson had sent up the coast on William Jardine's instructions in February; he was several hundred chests short of what he had promised. He was only spared acute embarrassment by the opportune arrival of a shipment of 500 chests assigned to Dent & Co. which he immediately bought at the full invoice price. Out of the total he had pledged to surrender, the share from Dent & Co. amounted to 6,000 chests. Jardine, Matheson usually commanded about one third of Canton trade and their contribution was 5,230. [43]

How on earth had Captain Elliott persuaded the Hong merchants to agree to surrender up what was in effect their capital wealth? Entirely on his own authority, stretching his 'plenipotentiary' powers way beyond their limit, he undertook that the British Government would compensate any losses to the tune of $9 million or about £2 million! This was putting a value of almost $450 on each chest at a time when sales were virtually impossible at any price. The opium traders could not believe their luck. Without having to haggle or bargain, they had been guaranteed a most satisfactory profit.

The stocks were duly delivered to Lin at Humen, an inlet off the Pearl River below the Bocca Tigris and the Bogue fort, where Lin had a number of channels dug and into which the opium was thrown, covered with salt and lime, trampled underfoot and then discharged into the river. [44] **[Plate 65]** When about three-quarters had been surrendered, Lin announced that normal, legitimate trade could resume. There was a scramble to offload the remaining woollen and cotton goods and take on board the season's tea crop. By July 4, the entire British community had decamped to Macau and Elliot applied for permission for British ships to resume trading from there. Lin curtly refused and ordered him to devise a plan for putting a stop to the opium trade up the coast and force the smugglers to sign the bonds he had prepared. Elliot knew this was quite impossible and he 'tore them up into a thousand pieces'.[45]

Enraged by this further display of defiance, Lin now sent a large body of troops to besiege Macau while at the same time, as he had in Canton, ordering all Chinese servants to leave their British masters and every Chinese shop to deny them food. The siege of the factories had been one thing; here in Macau there were whole families with women and children as well. The community was on the verge of panic. The renowned though somewhat eccentric painter George Chinnery feared that there was going to be a repeat of the 'Black Hole of Calcutta' massacre of 1756. He dropped a note round to James Matheson. 'I feel it is certain that something serious if not dreadful is coming and I am in a state of anxiety beyond expression. I ran down to the doctor the other night in fear and trembling. I do not go out again until I cross the beach.' Every British ship was mustered in the harbour for a prompt evacuation. Elliot posted a rather hysterical letter to Lord Palmerston describing 'protracted outrage ... spoliation of the very worst description .... the most shameless violences which one nation has ever dared to perpetrate against another.' [46]

The action now moved 40 miles east across the Pearl River estuary to the anchorage off the rocky, barely inhabited island of Hong Kong. Here a considerable fleet of shipping with inbound cargo for Canton had already assembled while the trade embargo was in place. Their numbers were soon increased by the evacuees from Macau. They had escaped one danger; almost immediately they would face another.

On July 7, a group of English sailors had landed on the Kowloon Peninsula in search of provisions and any form of activity to relieve the monotony of their confinement on board ship. In the village of Jianshazui they found a store of locally brewed rice liquor, proceeded to get very drunk and then get involved in a hefty brawl with the locals. A Chinese villager by the name of Lin Weixi died of his wounds the following day. This incident sparked two very different reactions in the two leading actors in the unfolding drama of Anglo-Chinese relations. Commissioner Lin demanded that the offenders should be handed over for punishment under Chinese law, a law that demanded 'a life for a life'. Elliot held a court of inquiry, fined the guilty parties and ordered them to be shipped back in due course to serve a prison sentence for manslaughter, not murder, in England. He also, out of his own pocket, paid $2,000 to the relatives of the deceased. This was British justice in action. Firm but fair punishment for the guilty – compassionate compensation for the victim. He was also very mindful of a somewhat similar incident that had occurred back in 1784 when an EIC ship, the *Lady Hughes,* had fired a ceremonial salute that went slightly wrong. A Chinaman in a nearby boat was killed by a piece of flying wadding. This was clearly a complete accident, but the Chinese authorities had demanded that the luckless gunner should be handed over for trial. He was then summarily executed.

Lin took Elliot's action as merely another example of the perfidious foreigner's resort to bribery to achieve his purpose. Basking in the Emperor's approval – he had sent Lin gifts and promises of promotion, writing that 'the affairs had been well managed' – he ordered three junks to move against the British ships and arrest the offenders by force. His informers may have told him that the sloop HMS *Larne* had been sent back to England with despatches in May, leaving the British ships with no naval protection whatever. He was confident that he was about to inflict a crowning humiliation on 'the red-haired barbarians'. As luck would have it though, on August 31 two ships of the Royal Navy had turned up at Hong Kong; the 18 gun sloop HMS *Hyacinth* and the 28 gun, 'sixth-rate' battleship HMS *Volage*. A few shots persuaded the approaching war-junks to scuttle back to harbour.

Notable absentees from the shipping off Hong Kong were the opium clippers of Jardine, Matheson. Their operations had shifted to Manila in the Philippines under William Jardine's nephew Andrew. The price of opium had slumped since Lin's appointment and James Matheson took full advantage of this to buy up every chest he could in Singapore, at prices as low as $150. That autumn his clippers were continuing to do a roaring trade up the east coast of China, and he managed to sell his investment of £40,000 at a profit margin of 200%. When news of Lin's destruction of the Canton opium stocks had first filtered up the coast, selling prices briefly hit a record of $3,000 per chest. [47] (Dent and Co. were probably doing much the same but, unlike those of Jardine, Matheson, their records have not survived.)

Elliot's actions now vacillated almost daily between reconciliation and aggression. When the Chinese captured and burned a Spanish ship in Macao harbour (in mistake for a British opium runner) he ordered the fleet to prepare to leave for Manila. Then he approved a scheme put forward by Captain Smith of HMS *Volage* for blockading the Pearl River and effectively putting Canton under siege, only to rescind it a week later and reopen negotiations with Lin for the resumption of normal trade. But some British traders jumped the gun and sailed straight up to Whampoa before this new agreement could be ratified. Lin had finally had enough. He reinforced his troops outside Macau and gave orders for the destruction of the shipping off Hong Kong by the Chinese navy.

The Chinese Admiral Guan set sail at the head of a fleet of 29 war junks and fire boats and on November 3 he passed the Bogue fort heading south for the open sea, a course that would take him very close to the two warships of the Royal Navy. As Elliot wrote later to Lord Palmerston, 'Captain Smith did not feel himself warranted in leaving this formidable flotilla at liberty to pass inside him at night .... and thinking that the retirement of His Majesty's ships was not compatible with the honour of the flag .... he made the signal to engage.' [48] The action that followed was fierce, brief and very one-sided. Within three quarters of an hour, at least three Chinese vessels had been sunk and several others had become completely waterlogged. Admiral Guan, severely wounded, ordered his force to retire. On seeing this, Captain Smith also disengaged and set sail for Macau. British casualties amounted to one sailor being slightly injured.

Lin's account of the 'engagement at Chuanbi' that he sent to Peking was very different. 'As the British ships shortly tried to flee the scene, the Qing navy decided to let them limp off.' [49] The Emperor wrote on the report, in red ink, that the engagement had been 'outstanding'.

Chapter 8

Palmerston goes to War

War makes rattling good history, but peace is poor reading.
Thomas Hardy

Lord Palmerston received the news about the engagement at Chuanbi in early February 1840. Mail between China and London was still taking four months even though the 'overland' route, exploiting the new rail links across Egypt and up through France, had reduced the total transit time considerably. William Jardine had been briefing him since his return to England and now his long report on the situation in China, with his own conclusions, became Palmerston's blueprint for a military campaign. In Parliament he argued that no other solution was honourable; British citizens, including women and children, had not only been insulted but confined and submitted to gross indignities. Their very lives had been threatened. Furthermore, the principle of Free Trade must be upheld; particularly in respect of tea. If this trade could be cut off at the whim of some Chinese potentate, might there not be civil unrest on the streets of London?

Palmerston was appalled by Charles Elliot's commitment to the opium traders about compensation and made it another of his stated war aims that the Chinese would have to be made to pay this. Opium lay at the heart of another of his debating points. In Britain, opium was used primarily for its medicinal benefits and occasionally by the intelligentsia for artistic stimulus, but addiction was unknown. What could be a greater contrast in moral probity than a nation like the Chinese where addiction was, if not completely universal, rife throughout all levels of society? Missionaries had already been quick to latch on to this practical example of relative godlessness, and now Palmerston could exploit it to persuade reluctant Members of Parliament to accept a military intervention 'for the good of the Chinese people', even at the point of a bayonet. As recently as 1832, a select committee of the House of Commons concluded that 'it was inexpedient to relinquish the revenue arising from the cultivation of opium in India for the supply of the market in China.' [50] But by concentrating on the 'cultivation', they omitted to mention the vital role played by Lancelot Dent and his fellow 'smugglers' to provide the link that made the argument an economic reality. And the economic scale can be quantified by the fact that the total revenues raised by the opium trade represented 10% of the Exchequer budget. [51]

There were heated debates in Parliament. William Gladstone, then a firebrand orator for the Tories, declared his opposition to 'a war more unjust in its origin ..... I do not know and I have not read of. The right honourable gentleman opposite spoke of the British flag waving in glory at Canton. That flag is hoisted to protect an infamous contraband traffic.' Finally the house divided on April 7 and Palmerston won approval for Britain to go to war with China by five votes. This clash between two over-confident nations has acquired the sobriquet of the 'First Opium War' with opium being the 'cassa belli', though as John Quincy Adams the former US President pointed out; 'opium was a mere incident to the dispute, and no more the cause of the war than the throwing overboard of tea in Boston harbour was the cause of the North American revolution.'

Who could Palmerston put in charge of this adventure? He was cross with Elliot but at the same time he recognised that no other person had his experience or local knowledge. On balance he felt that he had done as well as he could in the circumstances, combining reasonable arbitration with an appropriate use of force, particularly given the slender naval resources at his disposal. He had been high-handed and had overstepped his authority on occasions and at times he had shown lamentable indecision, but he had also proved his own personal courage. A bounty of $100,000 had been placed on his life yet he had survived. Given the short notice, Palmerston concluded that there was no better man for the job and on February 20, 1840, Captain Charles Elliot was confirmed in his appointment as 'Plenipotentiary', along with his cousin Admiral George Elliot. James Matheson wrote to William Jardine on April 26 in some dismay, predicting that 'the golden days of the (opium) trade were over.' In this instance he would be proved wrong again.

On July 4, 1840, a British expeditionary force of 22 warships, 27 transport ships and 4,000 troops arrived at Zhoushan island which lay off the north-eastern coastline of China's most prosperous region of Zheijiang. [See Map 6.] It was the gateway to the estuary that led up to the city of Hangzhou, the focal point for the distribution of food to Nanking via the Grand Canal and thence to the Imperial capital at Peking (Beijing). It had been on the advice of William Jardine that Palmerston had ordered the bypassing of Canton and the setting up of a blockade at this point on the coast several hundred miles to the north-east. (In May he had issued an edict that all Chinese merchant shipping could be seized and the cargoes sold to help pay for the campaign.) [52] If they were now not exactly on the Emperor's doorstep, they were only five days away by courier rather than the thirty two that it

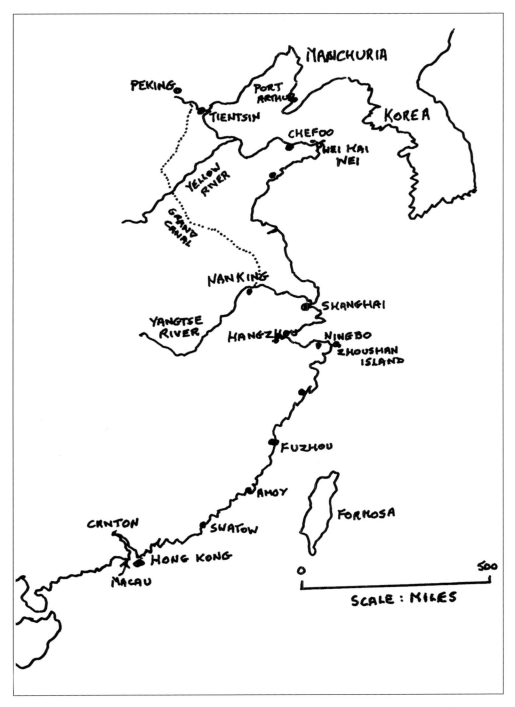

Map 6. Sketch map of the east coast of China showing key locations during the first opium war and the Treaty Ports. Also Peking and Wei-Hai-Wei.

took letters from Canton. Elliot's first priority at Zhoushan was to meet the local mandarins and persuade the regional Governor in the city of Dinghai to forward a letter to the Emperor containing the British Government's demands. The nub of these demands were fourfold; a complete and open resumption of trade, not only through Canton but at a number of other ports up the eastern coast; the cessation to Britain of a permanent trading base such as Hong Kong; ambassadorial representation on the basis of equality, not as supplicants, and several million dollars in compensation, not only for the goods that had been confiscated by Lin but also to cover the British Government's cost of going to war. To apply pressure, and allow the soldiers to disembark, Elliot requested the unconditional surrender of the island by the following morning.

In reply, the Governor said that he was far too frightened to dare to forward any missive to the Emperor, adding rather pathetically that it seemed unfair that they were being involved in a matter caused solely by the Cantonese. 'We see your strength and know that opposition will be madness, but we must perform our duty (even) if we fall in so doing.' It had become a matter of honour, of 'not losing face'. At 8 am, fifteen British warships were lined up against twelve Qing war junks. Elliot extended the deadline on his ultimatum until the afternoon hoping that sense would prevail, but at 2.30 pm his patience ran out and he ordered the British ships to open fire. Nine minutes later all the junks had been destroyed, the waterfront of the city reduced to rubble and the inhabitants sent fleeing into the hinterland.

Elliot now sailed further north still, to the city of Tientsin, only two hours from the capital Peking itself. Meanwhile the Emperor had received encouraging news from Lin in Canton. Some British ships, which he mistook to be returning opium runners rather than Elliot's battle-fleet, had paused briefly off Macau in June and had, he wrote, been driven off after 'thirty six vessels had been burnt and countless English killed'. This was a complete fiction but the Emperor recorded that 'he could not be more delighted'. He was not so pleased to receive notification on July 20 about the debacle at Zhoushan. He summoned the regional Governor responsible for Peking, Qishan, and ordered him to put his army on alert and strengthen fortifications. If the 'barbarians' appeared hostile, he was to annihilate them. The Emperor was somewhat confused when told that all they seemed to want to do was to deliver a letter. Why had he not been informed sooner? He ordered Qishan to make contact, accept the letter and forward it immediately to Peking. This meeting took place at Tientsin on August 13. Qishan told Elliot that he and his forces were now honoured guests and he even provided 'a liberal supply of bullocks, sheep and poultry'. Elliot's letter would be forwarded to the Emperor but a reply would take at least ten days. The British were invited to spend the time admiring the scenery.

Daogong's reply only addressed the British complaints against Commissioner Lin. Qishan delivered it to Elliot during a six-hour conference combined with a lavish banquet, generous gifts to his 'honoured guests' and much flattery. Lin had clearly misunderstood his commission from the Emperor and had obviously behaved very badly. He would be replaced, and so perhaps it would be best if the British were to withdraw and return to the area of Canton where further, constructive negotiations could take place in the same sort of cordial atmosphere? This flattering approach caught Elliot off guard. His honour as an officer and a gentleman could hardly allow him to go immediately on the offensive again and so he quietly withdrew most of his forces and headed for Macau. The Emperor was delighted with the outcome and amazed to find how easy it was to treat with these strange British people, whose Government had declared war on his country. They could probably be bought off with the right amount of silver. For a short time Qishan also basked in his diplomatic skill, though he was not so delighted when he was ordered to get down to Canton as Lin's replacement and be responsible for concluding any outstanding matters on the agenda. He was certainly not going to hurry down to take up his new appointment; he was shrewd enough to realise that it could turn out to be a hornet's nest.

At the end of his fifty-six day saunter, he recruited an eccentric young man as an interpreter, Bao Peng, who claimed to have been learning English all his life. In fact he only spoke pidgin English and what he knew of that had been acquired while working as a servant for Lancelot Dent! [53] Now, to the amusement of the merchants in Macau, he was turning up as a senior member of the Chinese delegation, wearing a buttoned cap, a rich satin robe and boots to match. Like the boatmen who disobeyed their orders and fell over themselves to bring provisions to Elliot's fleet on its arrival off Hong Kong in late November 1840, he owed no ideological loyalty to the Qing and would serve the master who paid the most. 'You thinkee me one smallo man?', he spluttered to his ex boss, going on to imply that in his hands lay the balance between peace and war.

Lin had made use of the hiatus to bring up more soldiers and recruit several thousand militiamen. He hastily constructed new forts along the banks of the Pearl River and reinforced the existing ones, particular at the Bogue. Soldiers were crammed so tightly into these forts that living conditions became unbearable and he had to pay out enormous bribes to persuade them to stay at their posts. Fatally as it turned out, all the ancient artillery pieces pointed out towards the river. And now he was curtly informed that he had been demoted and replaced by Qishan, who had once been a junior official on his staff. He withdrew himself to sulk in Canton.

Negotiations with Elliot were resumed on November 29 and lasted three weeks. Agreement was reached on the question of 'equality' in diplomatic representations but the giving over of Hong Kong was declared unthinkable. Elliot even dropped the demand for trading access to ports up the coast if trade could be resumed through Canton; this was rejected as impossible while the British still occupied Zhoushan. The Emperor's instructions to Qishan were to stall for time. 'When prolonged negotiation has made them weary and exhausted, we can suddenly attack and thereby subdue them.' Elliot issued a warning that he intended to go on the offensive on Boxing Day, then extended his ultimatum to January 7 when he finally lost patience once again and ordered the battle fleet to sail up the Pearl River.

Their first move was to land 1,400 marines, with field artillery, at Chuanbi and attack the fort there from the landward side. Forty-five minutes later the occupants fled and the Union Jack flew on the ramparts. The following day, Admiral Guan requested a ceasefire and the resumption of new talks. On January 21 Elliot resubmitted his terms for a treaty while Qishan begged for more time to consider his new instructions from Peking. These, in essence, ordered him not to communicate with the invaders in any way at all and to launch a 'punitive mission to suppress them'. War was resumed on February 25. The British troop moved on to surround the Bogue fort while it was pounded to destruction by the Royal Navy's newly arrived 'secret weapon', an iron-clad paddle-steamer appropriately called HMS *Nemesis,* armed with two pivot mounted 32 pounder guns and four six-pounders. The slaughter was appalling. Lin's insistence that the forts should be packed full of soldiers meant that those who were not blown to pieces and tried to flee were crushed to death in the narrow exits.

Elliot's fleet then proceeded upstream to take out each fort in systematic succession – the forts of 'Eternal Peace', of 'Consolidated Security', of 'Over-awing' and of 'Quelling Those From Afar'. The commander of the last informed his attackers that, to save face, he would fire six cannons before he ran away, but they would be blanks. Anyway, the Chinese were running out of saltpetre so their gunpowder was becoming less and less effective. Admiral Guan had been holding back his fleet of war-junks for a last ditch counter-attack in defence of the city of Canton itself, knowing that the river there was too shallow for the traditional British warships. But he was totally unaware that HMS *Nemesis* had a very shallow draught of only 6 feet and it had sailed up a creek round the south of Hanan Island and was threatening to attack him from his rear. He ordered his junks into action, but now *Nemesis* unleashed its next surprise, a battery of Congreve rockets. These screaming missiles shrieked their way to their targets and Admiral Guan could only watch in horror as his junks blew up around him and sank. **[Plate 61]** By the middle of March, Elliot was back at the factories. Qishan had already left, dragged away in chains to stand trial for betraying the Emperor's trust. Alongside him was the bumptious little Bao Peng, accused of spying for the enemy, and whereas Qishan's sentence of banishment was soon commuted Lancelot Dent's 'little pet' was condemned to 'death by a thousand cuts'.

Qishan's immediate successor at Canton was the aged Yang Fang, an army officer with an impressive record of crushing border rebellions. While he considered how to placate the Emperor on the one hand and try and work out why the British were so successful – he concluded that they must be using 'magic powers' – he allowed trade through the factories to resume. Houqua and other members of the Co-Hong greeted their counterparts like old friends. Merchant shipping of all nations started streaming up and down the river; vast quantities of tea, up to half a million pounds a day, were exported. To the delight of Lancelot Dent the opium trade resumed with renewed vigour.

Then another Chinese General arrived, the Emperor's own cousin Yishan, accompanied by a further 17,000 troops to defend the city, most of whom were exhausted, underfed and undertrained. The civilian population of Canton, except for those intent on looting, had fled inland.

On May 20 Elliot was informed by one of his spies that something was brewing and he suggested that the factories should be evacuated. That night, Yishan launched his stealth attack on the British shipping, floating a convoy of chained-together fireboats downstream on the ebb-tide while cannons on the city walls opened up a bombardment. It was a still night without the trace of a breeze but once again HMS *Nemesis* wreaked complete havoc, steaming backwards and forwards to pour a lethal fire against the unarmed, blazing junks. When the tide turned, the fire-boats, those that had not been sunk, drifted back upstream. They came to rest against the wooden buildings of Canton's southern suburbs which immediately burst into flames. Yishan's attack had been so 'stealthy' that he had even kept it secret from Yang Fang whose army had been supposed to launch a simultaneous ground attack. This force of about 8,000 soldiers now withdrew inside the city walls.

It was now the British turn to go on the offensive. A 2,400 strong force was landed to the west of Canton and by the evening of May 26 they had captured the hill forts to the north (the 'Fort of Extreme Protection' and the 'Fort of Extreme Security') and mounted their own artillery, aiming it at the heart of the city. There had been casualties though, higher than any in the war so far, and General Gough was determined on revenge. His orders were to open fire at 7 am. A few moments before that time, however, a lieutenant came panting up to his position and announced that Captain Elliot had ordered an immediate truce having finally got the Chinese to agree the terms laid out on January 20th. By the treaty known as 'the Convention of Chuanbi', Hong Kong was given over to the British, six million dollars would be paid for the ransom of Canton, all Chinese forces would withdraw at least sixty miles from the city, unrestricted trade was acknowledged and the equality of diplomatic representations confirmed. In a final gesture of reconciliation, several hundred coolies were made available to drag General Gough's guns down from their hilltop positions and load them back onto the British ships.

Then the recriminations started. Palmerston was furious that Elliot had not achieved enough, while the Emperor raged that his officials had conceded too much. Elliot was recalled to London, given a dressing down and shunted to a consular position in the newly established state of Texas. From there he went on to be Governor of Bermuda, then Trinidad and finally St Helena, and he was given a Knighthood in 1856. But on the whole history has not been kind to him and his time in China is remembered more for his vacillations than his achievements, while his desire to avoid bloodshed and his pragmatic concessions were seen as signs of weakness. One man on the scene was more complimentary. In January 1841, James Matheson wrote; 'It was only Elliot's iron firmness (a quality for which the world has not given him much credit) and his unflinchingness in taking every responsibility that forced the business through against the most formidable obstacles.' [54]

Lord Palmerston refused to ratify the treaty that Elliot had agreed and he was replaced in China by Sir Henry Pottinger, assisted by Admiral Sir William Parker, a veteran from Nelson's campaigns. Their orders were to resolve the 'unfinished business', and during the operations of late 1841 the coastal ports of Amoy and Ningbo were taken with only minor opposition. Shanghai surrendered without a fight, but as the British forces moved further north in the spring of 1842, resistance became tougher and casualties rose. By August the British threatened the great city of Nanking and the Emperor Daoguang finally realised that the 'barbarians' must be appeased. Three ambassadors, Qiying, Yilibou and Zhang Xi, were despatched to Pottinger to sign a binding deal. Qiying had assured the Emperor that 'although the demands of the foreigners are indeed rapacious, yet are little more than a desire for ports and the privilege of trade. There are no dark schemes in them.' That month, on August 29, the Treaty of Nanking was signed with much ceremony on board the 74 gun battleship HMS *Cornwallis*. The date coincided with the Queen's birthday and a 21-gun salute was fired in her honour. Zhang Xi practically leapt out of his skin, believing that new hostilities had started and that he would be taken prisoner.

The treaty gave the British Government the promise of 21 million dollars to be paid over three years. Of this, 6 million was to compensate British traders for the stocks confiscated by Lin, confirmation of the deal struck by Elliot but not yet paid; 3 million for outstanding debts owed by the Co-Hong and the balance of 12 million as war reparations. The treaty also granted trading rights at five 'treaty ports' – Canton, Amoy (Xiamen), Fuzhou, Ningbo and Shanghai – legal jurisdiction over British residents and moderate tariff rates. Crucially it confirmed the transfer of the island of Hong Kong to British sovereignty in perpetuity. There was absolutely no mention of the word opium.

When news of the signing reached London, letters to *The Times* declared that 'the war had been a great and glorious thing' ... 'perhaps no circumstance in the history of Great Britain ever gave such universal satisfaction to all classes of society in this country.' The editor ruminated on the cost to both sides but drew parallels with a purging event two centuries earlier. 'Was not the fire of London in 1666 a good thing? Did it not lead to immense improvement?' The reaction in the Chinese court was less unanimous. Qiying thought he had achieved a triumph; 'everything difficult can become easy ... our offspring must be prosperous and great in the future.' Yilibu, who had been sick with worry during the ceremony, was alarmed that the opium problem had not been resolved and professed that 'the root of disaster has probably been planted and the poison will flow ceaselessly.' The jolly drunkard Zhang Xi merely recorded that he was delighted at still being alive; 'how enjoyable and fortunate this is!'

The Emperor sulked; 'you have all let me down – and the empire.'

Chapter 9

Hong Kong and the Peaceful Years

In June 1843 the Treaty of Nanking was formally ratified by Parliament and received the signature of Queen Victoria. She had initially been rather amused when told that she now had a new colony with such a funny name as Hong Kong. But in her diary she echoed the chorus of disapproval surrounding Charles Elliot, 'who had completely disobeyed his instructions and tried to get the lowest terms he could.' The final ratification at Government House in Hong Kong, attended by the three Chinese ambassadors, was turned into a great ceremony and banquet as Lord Saltoun, the military commander, recounted. [55]

> The commissioners came in their state sedan chairs (from the celebrated grog-shop, Britons Boast, at which they were lodged) and had arms presented to them and so forth. We then got rid of our full-dress toggery as soon as we could, for it was infernally hot, and at seven o'clock sat down to dinner, a party of fifty. The High Commissioner Qiying sat next to Sir Henry Pottinger ... I had the Tartar General next to me with Zhang opposite. They did very well with the soup and fish, but when it came to the meat they could not use the knife, so we cut it up into small pieces for them, I feeding the Tartar as if he had been a tame sparrow and they ate and drank enormously of everything. About 11 o'clock the mandarins went away in their chairs as jollily drunk as any three fellows I ever saw in my life. [56]

There were four sealed copies of the final treaty documents, half in English and half in Chinese. But un-noticed among all the jollification was a small discrepancy in Article 2 regarding the status of the British in the Treaty Ports. The English version, as intended, granting them and their families *permanent* residence rights, while the Chinese copies only mentioned *temporary* rights – eg within the trading season. [57] As each country tried to assert the terms of the Treaty according to their own interpretation, a festering resentment developed on both sides. There are, in retrospect, many similarities with the Treaty of Versailles in 1919; major issues remained unresolved and within twenty years war would flare up once again.

Palmerston was still ambivalent about the whole opium business. In June 1842, he had been presented with a petition from two hundred English merchants denouncing the opium trade as a hindrance to legitimate trade, but he recognised that it was 'too important as a source of official revenue to be abandoned lightly.' He clung to the hope that the Chinese would eventually make it legal and therefore taxable and capable of being regulated. (This would not happen until after the Second Opium War in 1860.) Afterwards any smugglers who tried to avoid paying duties could be hunted down. His instructions to the new Governor of Hong Kong, Sir Henry Pottinger, were to make it clear to the Chinese authorities that, until this happened, it was up to them to enforce their ban on their own people. 'If your people are virtuous, they will desist from the evil practice, and if your officers are incorruptible, and obey their orders, no opium can enter your country.' As far as the British were concerned, they must only trade through the treaty ports and must abandon dealing with any other harbours along the coast.

When Sir Henry Pottinger relayed this edict in a proclamation to all the Hong Kong merchants in October 1843, he tempered it slightly by adding that it would 'not be contrary to this prohibition should British vessels approach and anchor for safety ..... near the coast of China.' He was in a cleft stick. On one hand, until an efficient banking system was set up, he desperately needed the silver that the opium traders delivered to pay for his overheads in Hong Kong because the legitimate trade was largely conducted by barter. On the other hand the commanders of the Royal Navy patrol vessels had orders to enforce the Navigation Act, which empowered them to check that all merchant shipping had authorised port clearances and licences for any arms they carried. The opium clippers had neither, but had to have effective weapons to beat off pirates and defend themselves against Chinese law-enforcement junks. The Admiralty also relied on the opium fleet for surveying in-shore waters; when, for example, they later needed a survey of the Yangtse River, it was the clippers that obtained the information for them. Off the record, Pottinger told the opium merchants to keep away from the British naval units and never anchor anywhere near them.

British consuls were installed in the treaty ports and they took much the same attitude. Alexander Matheson wrote in September 1843 to his manager in the north; 'Captain Balfour, the consul for Shanghai, and Mr Thom, the consul for Ningbo, are particular friends of ours and will give our vessels as little trouble as they can but it will be advisable to keep entirely out of sight of these ports ..... You will of course oblige either of them by cashing their bills or otherwise.' [58]

The opium clippers were, in effect, providing the consulates with a banking service.

In April 1840, James Matheson had written to William Jardine that he feared 'the golden days of the trade were over'. Once again he was over pessimistic. After the Treaty of Nanking, the opium trade 'flourished as never before'. [59] Between 1845 and 1847 alone profits rose from $33.6 million to $42 million. [60] This contrasted with a contraction in legitimate exports to China between 1843 and 1848 while at the same time imports of tea had doubled in value, those of silk increasing by a factor of twenty. By 1854 the British balance of trade was £8 million in the red, rising to £9 million three years later. It was politically impossible to try and counteract this imbalance by limiting the import of Chinese goods into England because the duties raised paid for the costs of the Royal Navy. So there was nothing for it but to let the opium trade prosper. In 1843 Palmerston had even ordered the annexation of the Indian territory of Sind, partly to prevent other sources of opium threatening the monopoly of Bengal and Bombay. Whether he approved of it or not, and in spite of the increasing moral outcry by Victorian society, it was opium alone that kept the wheels of Empire turning. By 1856, it represented a quarter of all the revenue generated by British India.

The Government at Westminster required that every colony should at the very least be self financing and not a drain on the exchequer. The exploitation of minerals or agriculture did not apply to Hong Kong; its assets were its harbour, its growing population, both British and Chinese, and land that could be portioned up and sold. James Matheson had taken advantage of the 'Convention of Chuanbi' to erect the first warehouse on Hong Kong at the same time that British Troops landed at 'Possession Point' in February 1841. The first official land sales were organised in June that year and Jardine, Matheson and Dent & Co. both bid vigorously for the best sites, the former around East Point and the latter in the Praya Central area. They vied with each other to build the most imposing properties. **[Plate 66]** Along the waterfront itself wharves and *godowns* were built, so that very soon it had an appearance very similar to the factories in Canton. Dents added to their portfolio in 1848 when they acquired another prime site on Queen's Road, one that had originally been bought by Dadabhoy Rustanjee as Lot 5 in 1841 and which would later be converted into the luxury Hong Kong Hotel. General Soulton wrote in June 1842 of his amazement at the speed with which the settlement grew: 'This is the most singular place, for they tell me that last September it had not four houses and now they have a street nearly a mile and a half long, most of the houses finished and inhabited, good shops of every kind, a bazaar and an excellent covered market place .... all kept clean and tidy.' [61]

A racecourse was an early property development once the malaria infested swamp of Happy Valley had been drained and became a very popular centre for social activities. Sporting clubs, so essential in all British colonies, were quickly established

Plate 48. Capt. Edgar Dent KOSB (1863-1906), father of Ruth Dent and grandson of John Dent of Madras.

Plate 49. John 'Dog' Dent MP (1761-1826), partner of Child & Co., Bankers. (Later part of Royal Bank of Scotland.)

Plate 50. The foreign factories in 'Faqi-city' outside Canton, 1805. Prominent is the EIC building, later to become the Chamber of Commerce for the British merchants after 1833.

Plate 51. *'Trainlands' farmhouse, the original Dent property, from the rear.*

Plate 52. *'Flass House', as rebuilt by Lancelot and Wilkinson Dent in the 1850s.*

Plate 53. Robert Dent (1793-1835). Partner in the London firm of Rickards, Mackintosh, Law & Co. an East India, China and General Agency.

Plate 54. John Dent (1795-1845), senior civil servant in the Governancy of Madras.

Plate 55. Thomas Dent (1796-1872), founder of Dent & Co.

Plate 56. William Dent (1798-1877), civil servant with the EIC and latterly the superintendent of opium production at Patna.

Plate 57. Lancelot Dent (1799-1853), opium trader into China and key figure in the 'siege of the factories' and the start of the First Opium War.

Plate 58. Wilkinson Dent (1800-1886), partner of Lancelot Dent in Canton and later in Hong Kong.

Plate 59. John Dent Jnr. (1820-1892), son of John Dent of Madras and partner in Dent & Co., Hong Kong. A leading figure in the formation of the Hong Kong and Shanghai Banking Corporation (HSBC).

Plate 60. Alfred Dent (1844-1927), junior partner in Dent & Co. Hong Kong and Shanghai, later knighted for his services in extending British influence in North Borneo.

Plate 61. First Opium War. HMS Nemesis *(back right) destroying Chinese war junks. January 1841.*

Plate 62. An EIC opium drying shed and godown.

Plate 63. Waterwitch, *the pride of the Dent opium clippers, built at Kidderpore 1831 (painting by David Wilson).*

Plate 64. Dent's elegant paddle-clipper Ly-ee-moon. *Built by the Thames Shipbuilding Co., she arrived on the China coast in 1860 (painting by David Wilson).*

Plate 65. Commissioner Lin supervising the destruction of the opium stocks at Humen, 1839.

Plate 66. The magnificent Dent building in Hong Kong, part of which later became the luxury Hong Kong hotel.

Plate 67. The Dent fountain, Hong Kong, dismantled in 1934. The lions were adopted by the HSBC.

Plate 68. Lancelot Dent's mandarin style bed (now in Durham University Museum).

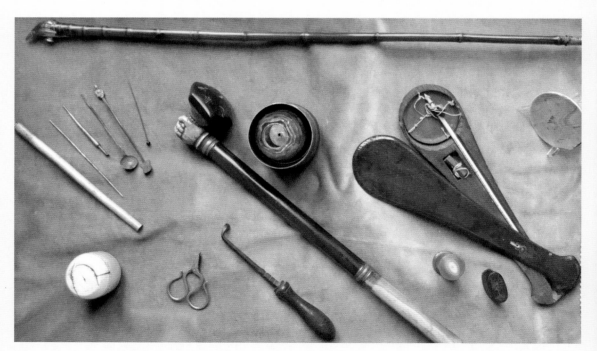

Plate 69. Opium smoking paraphernalia, including weighing scale, storage jar, lamp, pipe and prickers.

Plate 70. *The grave of Lancelot Dent, in the churchyard at Crosby Ravensworth.*

Plate 71. *Overend, Gurney and Co. share certificate issued in November 1865 as part of the despairing attempt to re-finance the bank. The issue was judged in many quarters to have been fraudulent.*

Plate 72. a) 'Bobjon', Ian Macnair's Bleriot Whippet cycle-car 1927. Ruth sits on the running board while the bemused locals look on.

Plate 72. b) Unloading from the ferry to the mainland.

Plate 72. c) Ian Macnair driving the Commissioner of Wei-Hai-Wei, Mr Johnson. (Later Sir Reginald.) He had been tutor to the last emperor of China, Pu-Yi, his role being played by Peter O'Toole in the eponymous film.

Plate 72. d) The Commissioner takes a spin at the Island Hotel.

Plate 73. The opening of the short-lived Shanghai-Woosung Railway, 1897.

Plate 74. HM Submarine L27 at Wei-Hai-Wei, 1927. Ian Macnair had the torpedo loading hatch enlarged during the boat's refit at Vickers the previous year so that he could stow the chassis, and all the other components, of 'Bobjon' on board for the long ocean voyage out to China.

Plate 75. One of the old defensive towers on the city wall of old Canton.

Plate 76. Watercolour by Ruth Macnair with the old walled city of Wei-Hai-Wei in the background.

Plate 77. A temple in the old city.

Plate 78. Street cobblers in the old city of Wei-Hai-Wei.

Plate 79. Ian Macnair (left) and brother officers on the golf-course, Wei-Hai-Wei island.

Plate 80. The Bund, Shanghai, photographed by the author in 2012. The building on the left, number 14, was built in the 1890s on the site of the Dent & Co. offices.

Plate 81. The daily opium ceremony in a village near Jodhpur in 2003, in which the author took part. A ball of raw opium is on top of the conical filter on the left-hand arm of the offertory with the 'loving cup' beneath.

and the first cricket ground was built in Happy Valley beside the racecourse. But this proved to be inconveniently far from the business centre and in 1851 advantage was taken of the army's new parade ground on reclaimed land by the Victoria barracks to lay out a new one close by. Rowing and sailing were particularly popular among young men and the Canton Regatta Club relocated to Hong Kong with John Dent Jnr. as its chairman. **[Plate 59]** He complained in a report that too many rowers were getting in the way of serious sailors, a protest that led to the foundation of the rival Victoria Regatta Club, the first club to allow Indian members. This in turn was split by internal rivalries, resulting in the breakaway Hong Kong Boat Club. Renamed later as the Royal Hong Kong Yacht Club, it was based on Kellet's Island where it remains to this day, the only institution to retain its 'Royal' title into the 21st century. (Golf, which required more space and better internal transport to flourish, followed in the 1880s.)

Away from sport and outdoor recreation, Hong Kong society was highly stratified, with the British *taipans* establishing a local aristocracy typified by the exclusive Hong Kong Club, which excluded 'shopkeepers, Chinese, Indians, women and other undesirables'. [62] Dents built a stately *taipan* house, 'Green Banks', on the slopes behind Central, a building that was later used as the residence for the Governor. They also paid for the erection of a clock-tower in Central and a magnificent fountain, flanked by four lions, which stood in what is now Chater Gardens. [63] **[Plate 67]**

The first Governor of Hong Kong, Sir Henry Pottinger was deemed to be too soft on matters of the colony's finances, too much in the hands of the merchants, and so he was replaced in 1844. His successor was Sir John Davis, an ex-EIC officer who had, for a very brief time, been the 'Plenipotentiary for Trade' in Canton after Lord Napier. So he knew the ropes and he believed that he knew what now had to be done in Hong Kong. Soon after his arrival, he announced new harbour charges and increased landing fees and sales taxes. These made him extremely unpopular but he then made matters worse by decreeing that all land sales were only leases for 75 years. This was to be applied retrospectively, so those like Jardine, Matheson and Dent & Co., who had bought plots in the sales of 1841 believing them to be freehold, were antagonised still further. All Chinese shop-keepers had to buy a licence and in 1845 he legalised the sale of opium in Hong Kong itself so that he could regulate the opium dens and turn them into another source of income. (It is a measure of Davis's unpopularity that when he put up a new Challenge Cup for a race at Happy Valley not a single horse was entered.)

Elsewhere, off the mainland, the opium trade accelerated. Jardine, Matheson had eleven receiving ships and six running ships off the coast and five crack 'clippers' to bring fresh supplies from India. Details of the Dent fleet are not so well documented but they were not far behind. In the ten months up to November 1845, opium exports from India amounted to 21,526 chests from Calcutta plus 18,321 chests of 'Malwar' from Bombay. [64] Three other nationalities contended as buyers, Americans, Parsees and Hindus, but the two British 'Hongs' dominated the market. On their return trips, the clippers were not only bringing silver but a whole range of goods. The manifest for one trip by *Waterwitch* in March 1845 included; 224 chests and 100 boxes of tea, 1,793 bags of alum, 50 chests of camphor, 126 cases of sago, plus single boxes of musk, fans, snuff bottles and assorted jewels. [65] The clippers provided by far the most regular and efficient transport links to Hong Kong and India, and thence to Europe, and were used as essential travel facilities for the British Consulates in the treaty ports both for passengers and even official mail. In 1847, for example, the consul at Ningbo requested that government dispatches were sent to him via Dent's offices in Hong Kong.

It has been estimated that in the decade from 1835 to 1845 the partners of Jardine, Matheson shared profits of around £2 million. [66] Again the figures for Dent & Co. are not known but were probably of the same order. Shanghai proved to be the most successful of all the Treaty Ports. The swampy area on the south bank of the river was drained and fitted with a reliable sewerage system, allowing the construction of offices and warehouses along 1,200 yards of what was originally called 'Bridge Street' but better known by its later name as the Bund. Plots were let out on 75 year leases with Jardine, Matheson taking the 3 acre lot 1 and Dent & Co. lot 8, which allowed them to build their offices at No. 14, the Bund. [67]

Perhaps the most significant change to the way that trade with China was conducted in the early 1850s was the introduction of steamships, and the arrival on the scene of the Peninsular and Orient Line. There had been one bold experiment with a steamer as far back as 1829 when Mackintosh & Co. had commissioned a steam tug from the New Howrah Dockyard with the idea of using it to tow a traditional sailing ship from Calcutta to Canton against the north-east monsoon. The *Forbes* registered 300 tons and her paddlewheels were driven by two 60 horsepower engines exported from Boulton & Watt in Birmingham. On March 14, 1830, the *Forbes* left Calcutta with the *Jamesina*, a 382 ton ex-Royal Navy sloop owned by Magniacs in tow. The coal for the journey was split between the two vessels, the *Jamesina* carrying 52 tons as well as her main cargo of 840 chests of opium. Making an average speed of about 6 knots, they reached Singapore on March 27, refuelled and left on March 31. Battling against the monsoon, speed slowed to only 3 knots, fuel consumption increased sharply and further delays arose from the need to tranship coal between the two vessels. They were not going to make it as a pair. So the *Forbes* cast off and headed for Canton on her own, arriving off Lintin on April 19, the *Jamesina* arriving two days later. When the captain of the *Forbes* picked up his Chinese pilot, he was amazed at the calm indifference shown by the pilot who explained that he had seen 'outside walkees' before, and that 'such a mode of propulsion had once been fashionable in certain ports of the Celestial Empire but had fallen into disuse.'

Only once later was this experiment with steam-power repeated by the British traders, when Jardine's brought out a small 58 ton schooner-rigged paddle steamer from Aberdeen in 1835. It was named the *Jardine* and was intended to speed the transit of passengers and mail between Canton and Macau, but the Chinese authorities refused to give it a river licence. [68] The cost of importing coal was another problem, so the matter was not pressed at the time and the introduction of the opium clippers proved to be a much cheaper and faster alternative.

By 1850, however, the situation had changed radically and the P & O quickly established a regular, reliable schedule throughout the Far East that creamed off the passenger and mail traffic as well as much of the cargo trade. Both Jardine, Mathesons and Dents were losing out to smaller, mainly American, rivals in the coastal opium trade and so both invested heavily in new designs of swift paddle-steamers. Jardines had *Riever* (778 tons), *Clan Alpine* (942 tons), *Glengyle* (1,266 tons) and *Glenartney* (1,088 tons), while Dents had a fleet that included *Fusiyama* (1,215 tons) and *Hirado* (1,294 tons), both used on the recently opened traffic up the Yangtse river. But the pride of their flotilla was the *Ly-ee-moon* (1,001 tons) that had been built by the Thames Shipbuilding Co. and arrived in 1860. Expensively appointed throughout, she was acknowledged as being probably the prettiest and fastest of all the steamers in the China trade. **[Plate 64]**

Chapter 10

The Changing of the Guard

During the 1840s the personalities within the two great 'Hongs' had been changing, with the 'old guard' of *taipans* handing over to the next generation.

William Jardine, while the opium war was raging in China, had been down at Ashburton in Devon, canvassing its 280 voters for his election as the Member of Parliament, rather than trying to win a wife in Scotland. He wrote to James Matheson on July 4, 1841. 'Thomas Dent laughed at the idea of my ever expecting to be returned,' enclosing a cutting from a newspapers that read; 'Mr McKillop and Mr Jardine canvassed Ashburton. The former, who boasted not a little of being certain of success, found it necessary to withdraw on the day of nomination and the latter was elected as a matter of course.' Lord Palmerston did not really believe that the rocky, barren, virtually uninhabited island of Hong Kong could possibly make a good trading post. He needed convincing. Now, as we have seen, William Jardine could persuade him, and the House of Commons, that its deep, protected harbour was a very valuable asset indeed, both for commerce and the Royal Navy. He handed over his partnership interests in China to his nephews David, Joseph and Andrew Jardine who soon moved the headquarters of Jardine, Matheson from Macau to Hong Kong in 1844. William Jardine's niece had married Thomas Keswick who was also invited into the partnership, and before long their son William would join them.

James Matheson returned to England in 1842 for the sake of his health, married a Canadian called Mary Jane Perceval and turned his attention to reorganising and revitalising, very successfully, the London banking firm of Magniac Jardine, renaming it Matheson & Co. His nephews Alexander and Donald became the working partners in China. His long time partner William Jardine died in 1843, still unmarried, and in the way that so-called democracy worked in those days his seat in Parliament was 'handed over' to James Matheson until 1847, when he was elected as MP for Ross and Cromarty, a seat that he held up to 1868. Before he left China, he had been purchasing property in Scotland and in 1844 he bought the whole of the island of Lewis for half a million pounds, there building Lews Castle and gaining the reputation of a philanthropic laird. He was knighted for his generous relief of the famine that swept the Outer Isles in 1851 but died childless twenty seven years later. (His title was resurrected for his nephew Alexander Matheson.)

It has already been mentioned that Thomas Dent had left China in 1830. On January 19, 1837, at the age of 41, he married Sabine Ellen Robarts at St. George's Hanover Square, an event that might have raised a few eyebrows since she was the step-daughter of his elder brother Robert Dent and 20 years his junior. Together they took up residence in 12 Hyde Park Gardens, an imposing house that overlooked Hyde Park, and the marriage would be blessed by no less than 12 children. Bringing up this large family may partly explain why Thomas Dent remained active in London commerce for many years including a directorship of the Royal Exchange Insurance Co. from 1858-67. Their third son Alfred Dent was born in 1844 and he was only twenty when he arrived in Hong Kong as a junior assistant at Dent & Co. in 1864. **[Plate 60]** Three years later he would find himself involved in the greatest crisis the firm had ever faced.

Lancelot Dent, who had been the senior partner in the Dent's Chinese operation since the departure of his brother Thomas, also left China in 1842 **[Plate 68]**, leaving his younger brother Wilkinson Dent in charge, together with their nephew John Dent, Jnr. Lancelot continued to take an active interest in the London end of the Dent operation, the merchant bank Dent, Palmer & Co., and a nephew recalled that he had attended 'the launch of LD's ship at Northfleet'. This ship, named *Northfleet* after the site of its construction, was a fully rigged 'Blackwall Frigate' of 895 tons that would spend its time taking cargo and passengers between London, India and Australia. (It was sunk by a collision with a steamer in the English Channel on January 22, 1873, with the loss of 320 lives.) He also retained links with his Westmorland roots, buying the Skersgill estate from his sister Elizabeth, starting the rebuilding of 'Flass House' in preparation for the eventual return of their brother Wilkinson and sitting as an Alderman for the town of Appleby. [69] Like his own uncle before him, he also played out the role of munificent benefactor by subsidising the education of some of his nephews. He died, very suddenly, in Cheltenham in November 1853 at the age of 54 and was buried in the family graveyard at Crosby Ravensworth. **[Plate 70]** By his hasty will, he left £40,000 in cash to various friends and nephews, plus his godson Rev. J Fish who was the son of one of the Dent clipper captains. The residue of his estate, including Skersgill, was bequeathed to his younger brother Wilkinson Dent, with power of attorney.

The year 1842 also saw Lancelot's brother William Dent resign his service in India after nearly 30 years and return to England, where he set up his own trading company alongside that of his brother Thomas Dent in London. Now his wealth increased substantially and he was elected to the board of the EIC in 1851, moving his family to the imposing Georgian mansion of Bickley Park.

Lancelot's third brother John Dent Snr. died suddenly in 1845, on a visit to Calcutta where he is buried. He had reached the pinnacle of his career in 1841 when he was appointed as the EIC's Provisional Member on the Council of Madras. It is in the cathedral of this city that his fine alabaster memorial can be seen, showing him dictating to his *munchee*. The engraved testimonial lists the details of his distinguished career and ends with a handsome eulogy. 'In private life, by his amiable and generous disposition, his overflowing kindness, his untiring zeal for the good of all classes and his high integrity of character, he won the hearts of all who knew him.' **[Plate 54]** But unlike many British *nabobs* who exploited their positions in India to make personal fortunes, John Dent Snr. did not die a wealthy man. By his Will he left everything he owned to his 'dearly beloved wife', to sell and convert into Government Securities, though he was worried that the income, after settling his numerous outstanding debts, would not be enough to support his wife and young family. He enumerates only one debtor – 'Mr Wellington of Griffiths & Co. owes me 12 dozen bottles of sherry.' In a codicil to the Will, he implores his sister and brothers to contribute to the education of his two younger sons at Haileybury. In fact both William McKerrell Dent and Robert Dent, my great-grandfather, left the school prematurely (the former for a disciplinary offence) and, instead of joining the East India Company, were bought commissions by their uncles into the elite Madras Cavalry. And he had further reasons to be concerned about his wife's future status and standing in the community because her father had gone spectacularly bankrupt in 1830. This cause celebre had even led to an Act of Parliament 'for the relief of the sufferers by the insolvency of Gilbert Ricketts, formerly Registrar of the Supreme Court at Madras.' Five years after the death of John Dent Snr., at the church of St George, Hanover Square, his widow Emily remarried a man called Charles Daniell whose family came from Helston Hall, Helston in Cornwall. Her brother-in-law and erstwhile trustee Wilkinson Dent was a partner in the firm of Daniell and Co. that traded into China in the 1830s and it seems more than likely that she had met her second husband through this connection. [70]

In the Celestial Court at Peking, the Emperor Daoguang died in 1850 at the age of 68. By then he had nine sons, four by the Empress and five, including the eldest, by consorts. Passing over his three elder children, Daoguang nominated the nineteen year old Xianfeng as his successor on the basis that he was not only legitimate but also the most intelligent. This sensitive young man would find his short reign dogged by war, internally by the bloody *taiping* rebellion in the south of the country and externally by renewed threats from the 'barbarian devils'.

Chapter 11

The Second Opium War

The flaws in the Treaty of Nanking became ever more apparent in the 1850s. Hong Kong was growing and prospering to a large extent but the basis of that prosperity was not built on sound foundations of increased trade. Unlike the thriving opium traffic, imports of British goods into China remained at a very low level. There was no access beyond the Treaty Ports themselves because the Chinese imposed crippling sales taxes and duties on all foreign goods moving inland. Individuals, including commercial travellers, were banned from travelling freely around the country and those who were either bold enough or dedicated enough to try their luck, like a few missionaries, often met fatal ends. Even in the Treaty Ports, relations with the local mandarins were undermined by the misinterpretations of the residency obligations mentioned earlier. There was still no diplomatic representation at the Imperial Court in Peking. Britain had gone to war with China in 1840 on the key issue of Free Trade and it was just not working.

Another problem for British trade was increasing competition from the French and the Americans, to whom China had also granted 'favoured nation' status by the treaties of Whampoa and Wangxia in 1844. These treaties, piggybacking on the hard won British Treaty of Nanking, were to a large extent similar but with one important difference – they could be renegotiated after twelve years. When Britain tried to extract the same concession in 1855 and presented modifications to the original terms, these were curtly rejected by the Celestial Court in Peking.

What is now known as the Second Opium War was triggered by an untidy incident in the Pearl River near Canton on October 8 the following year. Qing authorities boarded a trading vessel called the *Arrow* which they suspected of piracy and smuggling and arrested the Chinese crew. The ship was of Chinese design, a *lorcha*, and had been registered in Hong Kong, but the point at issue was whether it had been flying the British ensign at the time. If not, the Chinese authorities were within their rights; if it had, then the action was contrary to the terms of the Treaty of Nanking. The British consul, the sino-phobic Harry Parkes, believed the latter, seeing it as the ultimate insult to British authority. Since his appointment he had been seething with indignation that the Chinese still refused foreigners the right of entry, let alone residence, in the city of Canton itself. Attempts to enforce this aspect of the Treaty terms had already led to a succession of violent incidents and attacks on the 'factories', so Parkes used the *Arrow* incident as the excuse to call up naval and military forces to attack the Bogue forts and threaten Canton, an exact repetition of the events in 1839. This time the Chinese Governor, Yeh Mingchen, could offer no resistance because his troops were fully occupied trying to suppress a regional rebellion by a fanatical and increasingly militant cult, the *taiping*.

This cult consisted mainly of Hakka people who loathed the Manchu 'usurpers' and hoped to restore the old Ming dynasty, but also included mountain tribesmen and members of the Triad organisations with a similar agenda. The origins of the cult and the inspiration behind its leader Hong Xiuqan are bizarre. While studying in Canton to pass the stringent exams for a scholar's degree – essential for young men wishing to enter the civil service – he had read some Christian literature, doubtless translated by the missionary Karl Gutzlaff. He failed the exams for the fourth and final time, resulting in a complete nervous breakdown during which he suffered a series of delirious hallucinations, having visions of walking in the company of a paternal old man with a golden beard and a younger man who he called his 'Elder brother' and who gave him a sword with which to kill dragons. On awakening, his confused mind related the old man with the Christian God and furthermore his logic forced him to deduce that he, Hong, the 'Younger brother', must be the next Messiah. Now he set out to preach his warped version of militant Christianity coupled with a philosophy of abstinence from opium, a combination which seemed to offer a route to salvation by those trying to kick the addiction. By early 1851, he had recruited over twenty thousand converts and they embarked on a fanatical war-path, soon joined by peasants fleeing from the famine in Guanxi province. [71] (Their number rose to over 1 million by that autumn and over the next ten years the resulting civil war is reckoned to have cost over 20 million lives.)

Back to 1856, the British bombardment of Canton started on October 27 and continued until November 17 when Sir John Bowring arrived to try and re-open negotiations. But Yeh remained defiant, sending fire-boats to disrupt the British naval ships and managing to burn down all the foreign factories, except the British one, with incendiary shells. Admiral Seymour could destroy the wooden buildings in the suburbs but he realised that he did not have enough troops to storm the old city walls and a week later he withdrew all forces back to Hong Kong.

There the matter rested for a time while Britain became preoccupied with the Indian Mutiny and Lord Palmerston lost a crucial vote of confidence in the House of Commons on extending the conflict in China. Behind the scenes, however, he was

Postscript

In 2004, my wife Juliette and I made our fifth trip to India, tracing family roots and photographing wildlife. It was while we were looking for leopards near Jodhpur that I was invited to partake in the daily opium ceremony of the elders in a nearby village. We crouched on the earth floor surrounding a silver offertory dedicated to the elephant god, Ganesh, the god of good luck. A ball of opium was produced and placed on one arm of the offertory, prayers were intoned and a piece was broken off and placed in a conical muslin bag hanging off the other arm. **[Plate 81]** Boiling water was then poured in and a dark brown, pungent liquid dripped out into a silver cup beneath. When this was full, it was handed round with due ceremony, like a loving-cup, to each of the elders in turn – and then to myself. The taste was certainly like nothing I had ever encountered before, a sort of blend of fudge, pepper and over-stewed coffee. Under the slightly dreamy, glazed stare of the elders I let it slip down my gullet and waited for a mild hallucinatory experience. Readers may be disappointed to hear that I experienced absolutely nothing.

Endnotes and References

1   This disappointingly poor image, copied from Lubbock (see bibliography) is now the only one known to exist. It is a portrait, probably painted by Chinnery, once owned by the Dent family but sold at auction in 1972. The sale catalogue did not contain an illustration and I have been unable to trace the present owner.

2   Yorke p210.

3   Dormandy.

4   Ibid p111.

5   Ghosh.

6   ND.

7   Eneas Mackintosh was the uncle of James Matheson – see later.

8   Malayalum is one of the principal languages of southern India.

9   Lubbock p45.

10 Crisswell p21.

11 Lovell p51.

12 Conner.

13 An excellent description of this is given in Amitav Ghosh's book *River of Smoke*. Although an acknowledged work of fiction, the real names of the key participants, like Lancelot Dent and William Jardine, are used.

14 Crisswell p32. Raper's yacht *Fairy* capsized, drowning Captain Haddock.

15 Collis p79.

16 Low p544.

17 ODNB Philip K Law. The following quotations are also from this source.

18 Ibid.

19 Collis p218.

20 Yorke p217.

21 Yorke p217.

22 Yorke Appendix II.

23 Crisswell Appendix B.

24 Yorke p174.

25 Ibid.

26 In 1843, he became Secretary of Trade at Hong Kong.

27 Crisswell p44.

28 Yorke p218.

29 Yorke p215.
30 Baring Bros. archives.
31 Yorke p218.
32 Hoe & Roebuck p11.
33 Lubbock p152.
34 Lubbock p114.
35 Baring Bank archives.
36 Yorke p222.
37 Yorke p256
38 Baring Bros. archives.
39 Collis p218.
40 Yorke p229.
41 Foreign Office correspondence.
42 Lin to Elliot, March 1839, quoted in Yorke p231.
43 Yorke p428
44 A painting of this operation is printed in Lovell fig. 17.
45 Lovell p71.
46 Foreign Office correspondence.
47 Crisswell p60.
48 Foreign Office correspondence p468.
49 Lovell p94, quoting a Chinese biography of Lin.
50 Yorke p185.
51 Hanes & Sanello, p157.
52 Hanes & Sanello p106.
53 Lovell p126.
54 Yorke p462.
55 Yorke p343.
56 Yorke p344, quoting Fraser A, *The Frasers of Philorth*, 1879.
57 Lovell p247.
58 Yorke p453.
59 Yorke p457.
60 Chinese Repository, quoted in Lovell p251.
61 Yorke p478.
62 Crisswell p104.
63 Unfortunately demolished in 1934.
64 Lubbock p286.
65 Lubbock p286.
66 Crisswell p79.
67 Bickers p95.

68 Yorke p267.

69 ND.

70 ND.

71 Hanes & Sanello p167 et seq.

72 ODNB Richard Davenport-Hines 2004.

73 King p52.

74 King, pp167-9.

75 Crisswell p146.

76 Crisswell p106.

77 Crisswell p146.

78 Dent family papers, quoted in Lubbock p373.

79 Dormandy, p151.

80 Ibid.

81 Dent family papers.

82 The Shanghai operation seems to have closed down in 1875.

83 Macnair, Eleanor.

84 In fact her husband had confined her to a lunatic asylum.

85 This was a reference to the fact that they lived in Blackheath; nothing to do with any religious convictions.

Appendix A

Summary of Indian Indigo trade and UK Commodity trade with China

	INDIGO		OPIUM		TEA	Notes
Date	lbs.	Date	Chests.	Date	lbs.	
		1729	200	1750	12,000,000	
1782	26,000				[= £6 million]	
1802	4,400,000					
						1800-10 Net inflow into China $26 million
1815	7,650,000	1818	4,000	1820	c. 24,000,000	
1829	9,000,000	1834	30,000	1834	43,000,000	1834 Net outflow from China $3 million
						1828-38 Net outflow from China $38 million
		1838	40,000			
1847	11,000,000	1845	39,847	1848	86,000,000	
	[= 43,000 chests]	1859	51,000	1854		UK/China trade £8 million in deficit
				1857		UK/China trade £9 million in deficit
		1882	112,000			
				After 1860, tea trade shifts to Indian sources.		

Appendix B

Hills Family Tree

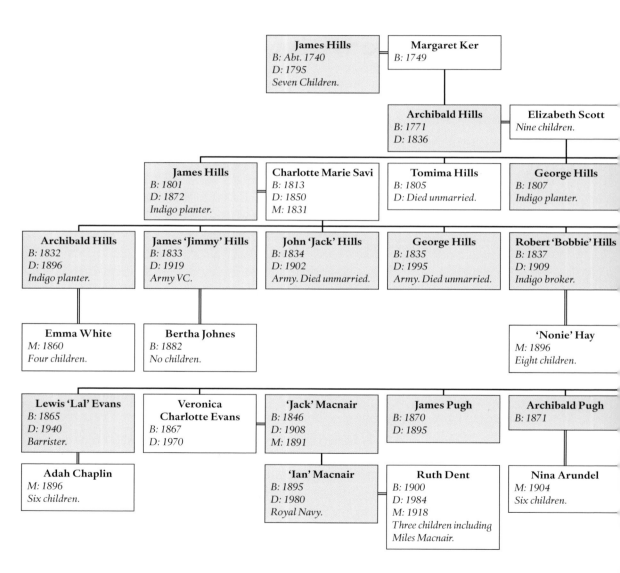

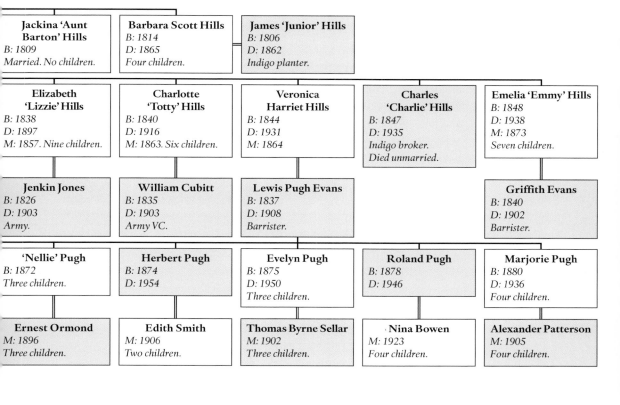

Jackina 'Aunt Barton' Hills B: 1809 *Married. No children.*	Barbara Scott Hills B: 1814 D: 1865 *Four children.*	James 'Junior' Hills B: 1806 D: 1862 *Indigo planter.*		
Elizabeth 'Lizzie' Hills B: 1838 D: 1897 M: 1857. *Nine children.*	Charlotte 'Totty' Hills B: 1840 D: 1916 M: 1863. *Six children.*	Veronica Harriet Hills B: 1844 D: 1931 M: 1864	Charles 'Charlie' Hills B: 1847 D: 1935 *Indigo broker.* *Died unmarried.*	Emelia 'Emmy' Hills B: 1848 D: 1938 M: 1873 *Seven children.*
Jenkin Jones B: 1826 D: 1903 *Army.*	William Cubitt B: 1835 D: 1903 *Army VC.*	Lewis Pugh Evans B: 1837 D: 1908 *Barrister.*		Griffith Evans B: 1840 D: 1902 *Barrister.*
'Nellie' Pugh B: 1872 *Three children.*	Herbert Pugh B: 1874 D: 1954	Evelyn Pugh B: 1875 D: 1950 *Three children.*	Roland Pugh B: 1878 D: 1946	Marjorie Pugh B: 1880 D: 1936 *Four children.*
Ernest Ormond M: 1896 *Three children.*	Edith Smith M: 1906 *Two children.*	Thomas Byrne Sellar M: 1902 *Three children.*	Nina Bowen M: 1923 *Four children.*	Alexander Patterson M: 1905 *Four children.*

Appendix C

Dent Family Tree

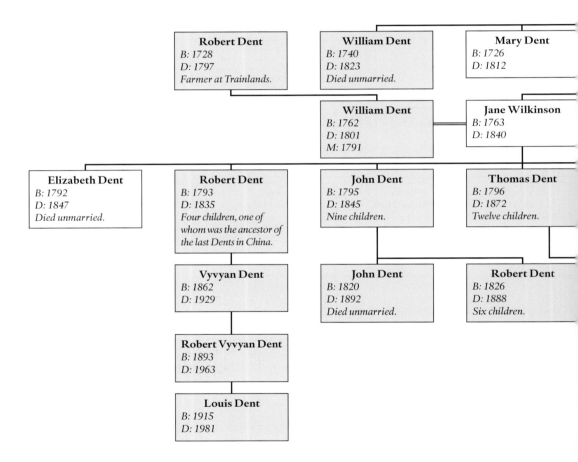

Robert Dent
B: 1728
D: 1797
Farmer at Trainlands.

William Dent
B: 1740
D: 1823
Died unmarried.

Mary Dent
B: 1726
D: 1812

William Dent
B: 1762
D: 1801
M: 1791

Jane Wilkinson
B: 1763
D: 1840

Elizabeth Dent
B: 1792
D: 1847
Died unmarried.

Robert Dent
B: 1793
D: 1835
Four children, one of whom was the ancestor of the last Dents in China.

John Dent
B: 1795
D: 1845
Nine children.

Thomas Dent
B: 1796
D: 1872
Twelve children.

Vyvyan Dent
B: 1862
D: 1929

John Dent
B: 1820
D: 1892
Died unmarried.

Robert Dent
B: 1826
D: 1888
Six children.

Robert Vyvyan Dent
B: 1893
D: 1963

Louis Dent
B: 1915
D: 1981

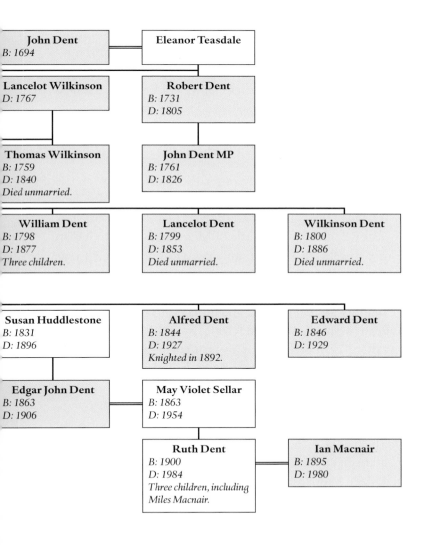

John Dent
B: 1694

Eleanor Teasdale

Lancelot Wilkinson
D: 1767

Robert Dent
B: 1731
D: 1805

Thomas Wilkinson
B: 1759
D: 1840
Died unmarried.

John Dent MP
B: 1761
D: 1826

William Dent
B: 1798
D: 1877
Three children.

Lancelot Dent
B: 1799
D: 1853
Died unmarried.

Wilkinson Dent
B: 1800
D: 1886
Died unmarried.

Susan Huddlestone
B: 1831
D: 1896

Alfred Dent
B: 1844
D: 1927
Knighted in 1892.

Edward Dent
B: 1846
D: 1929

Edgar John Dent
B: 1863
D: 1906

May Violet Sellar
B: 1863
D: 1954

Ruth Dent
B: 1900
D: 1984
*Three children, including
Miles Macnair.*

Ian Macnair
B: 1895
D: 1980

Appendix D

The Roxburghe Claim

Robert Ker of Cessford, which lies midway between Jedburgh and Kelso in the historic county of Roxburghe, was born in 1567 and was the man who first brought the news of Queen Elizabeth's death to King James VI of Scotland in 1603. He accompanied the King to London for his coronation as James I of England and held high office in the new court. He had already been elevated to the Scottish peerage as Lord Roxburghe in 1600 and in 1616 his loyal service to the monarch was rewarded by being created the first Earl of Roxburghe in 1616. When King James died in 1625, Lord Robert became the Lord Privy Seal to his son, Charles I.

Robert's ancestors had played key roles in the bitter in-fighting between the various border families, in the rivalries between the Scottish and English Wardens of the Marches and in the intrigues that surrounded the Scottish Royal court. His great-grandfather Andrew Ker was slain at the Battle of Melrose in 1526 by a man in the service of Lord Scott of Buccleugh as that family tried to rescue the 14 year old King James V from the custody of the Douglases. Andrew Ker's son (and Robert Ker's grandfather) Walter Ker avenged his father's death by murdering Sir Walter Scott of Buccleugh on an Edinburgh street in 1552 and is believed to have been one of the assassins of Mary Queen of Scots' secretary, Rizzio, in 1566. At the battle of Langside two years later, Walter Ker, together with his brother-in-law Lord Hume, led the Scottish Border spearmen in the critical action that resulted in Mary's defeat and her being driven into exile.

Robert Ker himself was no mean warrior at a time when the whole country was in the throes of the Reformation. At the age of 18 he fought to rescue the young King James VI of Scotland from the hands of the Earl of Angus and in 1590 he slew his cousin William Ker who had been appointed as the titular Abbot of Kelso. Three years earlier he had married Mary Maitland whose father had been the leader of the plot to murder Mary Queen of Scots' second husband Lord Darnley. Mary Maitland bore him a son, William, who died in France as a young man, and a daughter, Jean, who married John Drummond, the Earl of Perth, in 1613 and became the mother of four sons, the third of whom was christened William Drummond. Robert Ker married for a second time in 1614, this time to his first wife's cousin Jane

Drummond. To them was born a male heir, Harry Ker, who married Margaret Hay, daughter of the 10th Earl of Errol, in 1638. They then had three daughters; Jean, Anne and Margaret. If this all seems complicated, things will get even more complex when Harry Ker died in 1643 and the Roxburghe succession was thrown into confusion. In 1648, Robert Ker executed a Deed of Nomination naming his heir as his grandson, Sir William Drummond, to be followed, it was understood, by the male heirs of his 'eldest granddaughter without division'.

This deed was then ratified by an Act of Parliament. Robert Ker died in 1650 and, in accordance with an additional rider to his wishes, his granddaughter Jean married her first cousin William Drummond who could now become the 2nd Earl of Roxburghe, changing his name to Ker. William and Jean had two sons, Robert and John, who in turn both married and produced sons themselves, so the succession might seem to be secured. But before going any further we need to note for future reference Robert Ker's two other granddaughters; Anne, who married the Earl of Wigton (and their only daughter died without issue), and Margaret, who married Sir James Innes in 1666.

Robert Drummond-Ker became the 3rd Earl of Roxburghe on his father's death in 1675 but he only survived until 1682, when he was drowned while accompanying the Duke of York, later King James II, on his way from London to Scotland. The title passed to his elder son Robert, who never married and was in turn succeeded by his younger brother John in 1696. John, the 5th Earl, became Secretary of State to Queen Anne in 1704 and was created 1st Duke of Roxburghe for his services in 1707, 'with remainder to the heirs who should inherit the Earldom of Roxburghe'. On his death in 1740, the titles passed successively to his son (2nd Duke) and then his grandson John (3rd Duke), who died unmarried on March 4, 1804.

His was a rather sad story. As a young man, he had fallen in love with and became engaged to Christiana, the elder daughter of the Duke of Mecklenburgh-Strellitz. But when King George III came to the throne in 1760 and decided to marry the younger daughter, Charlotte, it was deemed undiplomatic for the elder daughter to marry any one and she remained a spinster for the rest of her life. Broken-hearted, John Ker devoted the rest of his life to literature and collecting antique books. With his death, all his English titles expired but the Earldom, being nominated as a Scottish title, then reverted to his distant cousin, William Drummond, 7th Lord Bellenden, who could trace his ancestry back to John Drummond, the younger brother of the 3rd Earl of Roxburghe. The 4th Duke did not, however, enjoy his new title and estates for long, dying without any surviving issue on October 23 the following year in his 78th year. Over five generations the House of Roxburghe had 'progressed quietly, without fuss, producing a succession of pleasant men with a penchant for books and one Duke in particular who collected one of the best libraries ever.'[1]

So who would the dormant title pass to now? This would prove to be a very thorny question indeed and one that would occupy the College of Heralds, countless lawyers and the House of Lords itself for seven years. There were four contenders who laid claim to the title; Lady Essex Ker, Sir William Drummond, Sir James Innes and my ancestor Brigadier-General Walter Ker of Littledean and Nenthorn.

Lady Essex Ker based her claim on being the sister of the 3nd Duke of Roxburghe, a claim that was quickly dismissed. As also was that of Sir William Drummond who, like his namesake the 4th Duke, based his claim on his descent from John Drummond, 2nd Lord Bellenden. But when the House of Lords considered the petition of General Walter Ker in February 1806, the matter was referred to the Committee for Privileges who finally got round to hearing evidence in June 1808. [2] Mr Erskine, Counsel for General Ker, argued that the terms of whatever had been arranged by the first Earl in 1648, allowing descent through the female line, should have applied *only* to the title of Lord Ker of Cessford, not the Earldom, and that attention should revert to the wording of the original Scottish letters patent appointing Robert Ker as the first Earl of Roxburghe in 1616. These had originally been thought to be missing, but Erskine had found them among the papers of the Macer's Court and they stated that the honour of the Earldom was 'limited to him and his heirs male'. And General Ker could trace his ancestry back to the 1st Earl through an uninterrupted line of male descent.

The matter was next brought to the House of Lords on March 20 1809, when a revised petition on behalf of General Ker was presented by Lord Liverpool. Their Lordships procrastinated yet again by referring it back to the Committee for Privileges who met a week later to consider the precise interpretation of the 'Deed of Tailzie, Nomination and Designation' executed by Robert Ker in 1648. This long, intricate document, written in antique Scottish, had ended with a clause that appeared to state that if the first condition about the sons of his eldest granddaughter, and their male heirs, should expire, then the title(s) should pass to 'our nearest and lawful aires maill q'fumevir'. Somewhat baffling. Unable to reach a decision, the committee adjourned – indefinitely. For the next three years, lawyers and genealogists for both remaining claimants produced thousands of pages of descendant charts and conflicting interpretations of the wording. This cost a lot of money. Sir James Innes was forced to sell his estate and General Ker not only had to mortgage Nenthorn and Littledean but also borrow money from his relations. His wife proclaimed the motto 'The Duchess of Roxburghe or a Beggar!' [3] Both men, now in their 70s, were gambling on the final outcome for very high stakes indeed. Sir James Innes's wife was barren, but when she died in July 1807 he promptly – the following week in fact – married again, this time to Harriet Charlewood, the daughter of Benjamin Charlewood of Windlesham in Surrey. She proved her fertility within a couple of years by giving birth to a daughter but the child died in infancy.

The legal stale-mate was finally broken by the presentation of another petition to the House of Lords on March 13, 1812. In this, Sir James Innes, now adopting the name Innes-Ker, claimed through his counsel Sir Samuel Romilly that the crucial wording about the 'eldest granddaughter without division' of the 1st Earl implied *the eldest granddaughter who survived*, and that meant the aforementioned Margaret Ker, who had married Sir James's Innes's great-grandfather in 1666. Their Lordships now agreed to concur with this interpretation and ruled on May 11, 1812, that Sir James Innes-Ker was now the rightful 5th Duke of Roxburghe. But with a qualification. In the absence of Sir James having a male heir, the title should then revert to General Walter Ker and his descendants. The first thing the new Duke did was to sell off the contents of the great library with all the books accumulated by the 4th Duke, one book alone that dated back to 1471 realising £2,260. The scale of the auction can be judged by the fact that it was spread over 45 days. [4] Duke James was now aged 77, so the General believed that it might not be long before his ruinous campaign might finally bear fruit and see him installed in the Roxburghe family seat at Floors Castle surrounded by its estate of 53,000 acres.

It was not to be. Four years later, the Duchess of Roxburghe announced that she was pregnant, adding that she was not going to endure her confinement within the chilly walls of Floors but in Paris. In July 1816, she duly returned with a healthy baby boy who, quite unlike the Duke, had very dark skin and jet-black eyes. An article in the 'Kelso Chronicle' for August 20, 1897, stated that 'the country gossip had it that this son was the child of a gypsy .... and that his dark complexion, so unlike the family in features, gave credence to the tale.' It is from this child that the present Dukes of Roxburghe are descended.

NOTES
1 Masters.
2 Journals of the House of Lords. Together with all subsequent extracts from their deliberations and rulings.
3 JJE. It seems that General Walter Ker married for a second time in 1797, a Jane Forster of Brunton, Northumberland.
4 Masters.

Appendix E

The Third Victoria Cross

In October 1917 Col. Lewis Pugh Evans found himself assigned from the Black Watch to command the 1st Battalion of the Lincolnshire Regiment, whose officer cadre had been decimated by the British offensives of that year. His citation gives a condensed account of his outstanding, and one has to say rather foolhardy, bravery.

"For conspicuous bravery and leadership. Lieutenant-Colonel Evans took his battalion in perfect order through a terrific enemy barrage, personally formed up all units, and led them to the assault. While a strong machine-gun emplacement was causing casualties and the troops were working round the flank, Lt. Col. Evans rushed at it himself, and, by firing his revolver through the loophole, forced the garrison to capitulate. After capturing the first objective, he was severely wounded in the shoulder, but refused to be bandaged, and reformed the troops, pointed out all future objectives, and again led his battalion forward. Again badly wounded, he nevertheless continued to command until the second objective was won, and after consolidation, collapsed from loss of blood. As there were numerous casualties, he refused assistance, and by his own efforts ultimately reached the dressing station. His example of cool bravery stimulated in all ranks the highest valour and determination to win."

Afterwards, he would come under some criticism from the upper echelons of the Army for putting himself, a Colonel, at unnecessary risk by 'acting like a green-horn subaltern', and in later life, he wrote a military paper in which he said that the commander should not leave his command post! For his services to his country, he was also awarded the CMG (in addition to his 2 DSOs), and for his 'exemplary behaviour in the cause of freedom', the Croix de Geurre and the Order of Leopold of the Belgians. [1]

NOTES
1   All Col. Evans' medals are now (2013) in the Ashcroft Gallery of the Imperial War Museum.

Bibliography

Anderson, A. *The Story of Ferniehurst*, 1934.

Balfour-Paul, J. *Indigo*, British Museum Press, 1998.

Bansal, U. & B. *Indian Journal Of History of Science*, 19 (3): 215-223, 1984.

Bickers, R. *The Scramble for China; foreign devils in the Qing Empire*, Penguin 2012.

Collis, M. *Foreign Mud*, Faber & Faber, 2008.

Conner, P. *The Hongs of Canton*, English Art Books, 2013.

Cotton, Sir H. *New India or India in Transition*, 1886.

Crisswell, C. *The Taipans; Hong Kong's Merchant Princes*, Oxford University Press, 1981.

Dormandy. T. *Opium; Reality's Dark Dream*, Yale University Press 2012.

Dubus, P. *Reminiscences of twenty years pig-sticking in Bengal*, Thacker Spink, Calcutta, 1893.

Everitt, D. *The K Boats*, Harrap, 1963.

Farwell, B. *Queen Victoria's Little Wars*, Penguin Books Ltd. 1973.

Fraser, G.M. *The Steel Bonnets; the story of the Anglo-Scottish border reivers*, Harper Collins 1995.

Garfield, S. *Mauve*, Faber & Faber, 2000.

Gastrell & Blauford. *Report on the Calcutta Cyclone of October, 1865*, Calcutta Orphan Press, 1866.

Ghosh, A. *Sea of Poppies* and *River of Smoke*, John Murray 2011. (Novels)

Hanes & Sanello. *The Opium Wars; the addiction of one Empire and the corruption of another*, Sourcebooks Inc., 2002.

Hoe & Roebuck. *The taking of Hong Kong*, Curzon Press, 1999.

Keswick, M. (edited). *The Thistle and the Jade*, Octopus Books, 1982.

King, F.H. *The History of the Hong Kong and Shanghai Banking Corporation*, Cambridge University Press, 1987.

Kling, B. *The Blue Mutiny; the indigo disturbances in Bengal, 1859-62*, University of Philadelphia Press, 1966.

Leasor, J. *Boarding Party*, Heinemann 1978.

Low, H. *Lights and Shadows of a Macao Life; the Journal of Harriet Low, Travelling Spinster,* Hodges & Hummel 2002.

Lubbock, B. *The Opium Clippers*, Brown Son & Ferguson, 1933 – reprinted 1967.

Macnair, Eleanor. (edited.) *China Wife*, Falcon Books, 1999.

Masters, B. *The Dukes*, The Book Service, 1975.

Washbrook, D. *Economic Depression and the making of Traditional Society in Colonial India (1820-1855)*.

The Register of the Victoria Cross, This England, 1997.

Unpublished

AH. *Diaries of Archibald Hills*, in the possession of his grandson, Archibald Chalmers-Hills.

CE. Notes compiled by Christopher Evans, great-grandson of Griffith and 'Emmy' Evans.

Greer, A. *Stories new and old*. Alice Greer (nee Evans 1875) was 'Emmy' Hills's second daughter and her memoirs consist of reminiscent sketches of various members of her family.

JJE. Memoirs of 'Jim-Jack' Evans, third son of Griffith and 'Emmy' Evans, b 1895.

LPP. Autobiography of Lewis Pugh Pugh, VHP's eldest son, 1935.

ND. Research by Nicholas Dent.

PM. Research by Phylidda Mould.

VHP. Memoirs, written for her grand-children 1917-1922.

Yorke, G. *The Princely House; The story of the early years of Jardine, Matheson 1782-1844*, written in the late 1930s but never published – at the request of Henry Keswick.

Film

The Opium War, directed by Jin Xie, 1997.

Index